THE WINNER!

John F. Kennedy, stepped up to the microphone on the last day of the convention to accept formally the mantle of candidacy.

"...The problems are not all solved and the battles are not all won—and we stand today on the edge of a New Frontier—the frontier of the 1960's—a frontier of unknown opportunities and perils—a frontier of unfulfilled hopes and threats...."

Kennedy paused, breathed deeply and concluded:

"It has been a long road...to this crowded convention city. Now begins another long journey, taking me into your cities and homes all over America. Give me your help...."

The crowd cheered.

"Give me your hand"—the roar became ear-deafening—"your voice and your vote."

YOUNG MAN IN THE WHITE HOUSE:
John Fitzgerald Kennedy
was originally published by
Julian Messner.

Critics' Corner:

"John Fitzgerald Kennedy comes through as a complex man, with courage only one aspect of his character. This is a book for the junior high and high school students for whom the spirit of the New Frontier was embodied by President Kennedy."
—*Young Reader's Review*

"A detailed and commendable biography...."
—*The New York Times*

"...an amazing level of objectivity."
—*Virginia Kirkus Service*

"...well-organized, well-written account...should prove to be inspirational to many of our young readers."
—*Library Journal*

Other Recommendations: Child Study Association; Bro-Dart Foundation, Elementary School Library Collection; H. W. Wilson Junior High School Library Catalog.

About the Author:

I. E. LEVINE is a native New Yorker who lives in Long Island with his wife and two children. During World War II he was a navigator in the U.S. Army Air Corps and flew thirty-two bombing missions over Germany and occupied Europe. After the war he completed his education at City College and also worked in the college's public relations department. He is now Assistant to the President and Director of Public Relations. "I enjoy writing biographies for young people," Mr. Levine says. "Each time I undertake a new subject it's like embarking on a new adventure. I consider it a challenge to try to convey my own feeling of adventure and excitement to the reader. Since we expect young people to meet the challenge of tomorrow, I think it is important for them to have a sense of the drama of history, as reflected in the lives of the important figures who helped mold the past."

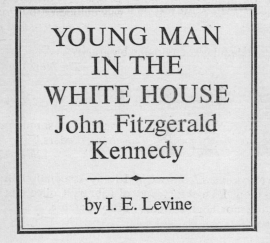

YOUNG MAN IN THE WHITE HOUSE
John Fitzgerald Kennedy

by I. E. Levine

AN ARCHWAY PAPERBACK
WASHINGTON SQUARE PRESS • NEW YORK

YOUNG MAN IN THE WHITE HOUSE
John Fitzgerald Kennedy

An Archway Paperback edition

1st printing .... April, 1969

Front cover photograph: Wide World Photos

L

Published by
Washington Square Press, a division of Simon & Schuster, Inc.,
630 Fifth Avenue, New York, N.Y.

WASHINGTON SQUARE PRESS editions are distributed in the
U.S. by Simon & Schuster, Inc., 630 Fifth Avenue, New
York, N.Y. 10020 and in Canada by Simon & Schuster
of Canada, Ltd., Richmond Hill, Ontario, Canada.

Standard Book Number: 671-29265-X.
Library of Congress Catalog Card Number: 64-20160.

To my wife Joy, with love

CONTENTS

YOUNG MAN
IN THE
WHITE HOUSE
John Fitzgerald
Kennedy

1

THE TORCH IS PASSED

The morning of January 20, 1961, dawned clear and cold. A biting wind knifed through the flag-bedecked streets of Washington, D.C. The city itself lay under a gleaming white blanket of snow. Reflected from the domed and turreted buildings of the capital, the glaring rays of the sun created a jeweled effect that seemed entirely in keeping with the ceremonial atmosphere.

Along the broad expanse of Pennsylvania Avenue more than a million people lined the street. They shivered good-naturedly as they waited for the parade that was to culminate in the inauguration of John Fitzgerald Kennedy as the thirty-fifth President of the United States.

The route itself had been cleared of the eight-inch snow which had fallen during the previous day and night. The blizzard—the worst the capital had seen in almost a decade—had dampened the Inauguration Eve festivities. However, just before dawn the snow had miraculously stopped falling. Now, in spite of the intense cold, a warm excitement gripped the city as the ceremony was about to get under way.

In front of the White House grounds, knots of people

clustered anxiously, straining to catch a glimpse of the dignitaries whose automobiles were entering the gates leading to the executive mansion.

Shortly after 11:00 A.M. a buzz of anticipation greeted the approach of a familiar vehicle. It was the presidential automobile, sent by retiring President Dwight D. Eisenhower to pick up his successor. Guarded by an escort of Secret Service men and city police, the car cleared the White House gate while the crowd caught a glimpse of the smiling, youthful President-Elect and his beautiful wife, Jacqueline.

The Kennedys, who had just come from church, were received at the portico of the mansion by President Eisenhower who came out bareheaded to meet them. They went inside together. A few minutes later the old and new Vice-Presidents, Richard M. Nixon and Lyndon Baines Johnson, and their wives arrived at the White House, followed by a number of Congressional leaders.

Within half an hour the entire assemblage emerged from the executive mansion, led by General Eisenhower and Mr. Kennedy who wore top hats. While they posed for news photographers and movie and television cameramen the President and President-Elect smiled and chatted together amiably.

At last they left the portico, accompanied by the Speaker of the House of Representatives, Sam Rayburn of Texas, and the Chairman of the Inaugural Committee, Alabama Senator John Sparkman, and headed for the first car. At that moment Mrs. Eisenhower and Mrs. Kennedy came out of the White House together and approached the second automobile. Mrs. Kennedy stepped back to allow the retiring First Lady to precede her into the vehicle.

Now the inaugural procession left the White House grounds and swung onto Pennsylvania Avenue to the accompaniment of the cheering people lined up along the sidewalks. The entourage slowly made its way along the parade route toward the Capitol in the distance.

Finally the procession turned onto Constitution Avenue and approached the great structure which, perched atop an eighty-eight-foot-high plateau like a jeweled crown, had served as the center of government of the United States for more than one hundred and sixty years.

Some twenty thousand people had massed in front of the East Portico of the Capitol where a stand had been erected for the ceremony. The long line of vehicles halted and the dignitaries emerged from their automobiles and were ushered onto the platform.

Mr. Eisenhower and Mr. Kennedy sat side by side. Nearby was another former President, Harry S. Truman. Occasionally, Mr. Eisenhower turned to Mrs. Kennedy to include her in the conversation. As the moment for the start of the proceedings drew near, it seemed to the spectators that John F. Kennedy became more and more taciturn. He listened to Mr. Eisenhower but seemed to be saying little in return.

The inauguration was now half an hour late, and the cold was bitter, but no one seemed to mind. The enthusiasm of the crowd seemed to increase instead of diminish.

At last Senator Sparkman advanced to the microphone to open the ceremonies. A hush fell on the crowd. Marian Anderson, one of America's leading contraltos, sang "The Star-Spangled Banner" in a deep, rich voice. Then tall, gray-haired Richard Cardinal Cushing of Boston, an old friend of the President-

Elect's family, delivered the invocation in a voice that
sounded harsh as it struggled against the wind.

Smoke suddenly began to curl around the feet of the
Cardinal. It came from a small electric heater that had
been placed inside the high lectern on the platform to
keep the feet of the speakers warm. Fearing a short
circuit, several officials discreetly approached, holding
buckets of water and fire extinguishers in readiness.
But the Roman Catholic prelate continued as if the
commotion had not even taken place.

Prayers followed by Archbishop Iakavos of the
Greek Orthodox Church, the Reverend Dr. John Bar-
clay of the General Christian Church of the Disciples
of Christ in Austin, Texas, and by Rabbi Nelson
Glueck, President of Hebrew Union College.

Robert Frost, the distinguished American poet
whom John Kennedy greatly admired, was to read a
verse entitled "The Gift Outright." The strong glare of
the sun and the stiff wind made it difficult for him to
read his poem, so, discarding the written text, he delivered it from memory in a firm voice.

"The land was ours before we were the land's.
She was our land more than a hundred years
Before we were her people. . . ."

Speaker Sam Rayburn administered the oath of
office to Vice-President Johnson. The moment had
arrived. . . .

Earl Warren, Chief Justice of the Supreme Court,
came forward. John Kennedy, who had removed his
top hat, now rose, slipped swiftly out of his overcoat
and placed his right hand upon the Bible, an old family
Bible that contained the genealogy of the Kennedys for

generations back. Standing grave and erect, he pledged himself in a solemn voice to uphold the duties of his new office.

Then, with scarcely a pause to clear his throat, he plunged right into his Inaugural Address.

Tall and slim, with youthful features and a shock of unruly sandy hair, he looked even younger than his forty-three years as he began to speak to the nation and the world. He spoke in a taut, somewhat high-pitched voice punctuated by the flat, broad accent of his native Boston.

"Vice-President Johnson, Mr. Speaker, Mr. Chief Justice, President Eisenhower, Vice-President Nixon, President Truman, Reverend Clergy, fellow citizens," he began. "We observe today not a victory of party but a celebration of freedom—symbolizing an end as well as a beginning—signifying renewal as well as change. For I have sworn before you and almighty God the same solemn oath our forebears prescribed nearly a century and three-quarters ago.

"The world is very different now. For man holds in his mortal hands the power to abolish all forms of human poverty and all forms of human life. And yet the same revolutionary beliefs for which our forebears fought are still at issue around the globe—the belief that the rights of man come not from the generosity of the state but from the hand of God.

"We dare not forget today that we are the heirs of that first revolution. . . ."

It was a ringing, eloquent introduction, a beginning that surprised many of those who had thought of John F. Kennedy as a cold intellectual without the instinct for passion or deep personal commitment. True, he had come close to eloquence in his speech at the Democratic national convention, following his nomination for the Presidency. But here, for perhaps the first time, he seemed to be talking from the heart.

The audience listened in rapt silence, their attention riveted on the coatless young man at the lectern.

". . . Let the word go forth from this time and place to friend and foe alike, that the torch has been passed to a new generation of Americans—born in this century, tempered by war, disciplined by a hard and bitter peace, proud of our ancient heritage—and unwilling to witness or permit the slow undoing of those human rights to which this nation has always been committed, and to which we are committed today at home and around the world. . . ."

John Fitzgerald Kennedy, the youngest man ever elected President of the United States and the first President born in the twentieth century, addressed himself to the young people of America—indeed to the youth of the world—in words that were to prove memorable.

". . . Let every nation know, whether it wishes us well or ill, that we shall pay any price, bear any burden, meet any hardship, support any friend, oppose any foe to assure the survival and the success of liberty.

"This much we pledge—and more. . . ."

The cadenced sentences and elegant austerity of language gave his words a simple, direct forcefulness. The speech could almost have been mistaken for classical Greek rhetoric.

President Kennedy talked about continued cooperation with America's friends and allies. He spoke of the need to relieve mass misery all over the globe, to launch a new "alliance for progress" aimed at helping the Latin-American republics to the south. He pledged to support the United Nations in its efforts. And he urged that the quest for peace begin anew, exhorting the nation never to negotiate out of fear—but never to fear to negotiate.

John F. Kennedy, first Roman Catholic President of the United States, pleaded with an almost religious fervor for help.

"I do not shrink from this responsibility—I welcome it. I do not believe that any of us would exchange places with any other people or any other generation. The energy, the faith, the devotion which we bring to this endeavor will light our country and all who serve it—and the glow from that fire can truly light the world.

"And so, my fellow Americans: ask not what your country can do for you—ask what you can do for your country.

"My fellow citizens of the world: ask not what America can do for you, but what together we can do for the freedom of man. . . ."

The eloquent words of the young President fell upon the assemblage with stunning impact. In the days and months that were to follow they would be quoted time and again. But for the moment, as the last applause died down, John Fitzgerald Kennedy sensed only that he had managed to move his audience profoundly.

The torch had been passed. A new era was about to begin.

2

ROOTS OF THE PAST

John Fitzgerald Kennedy had always evinced an awareness of the past. Even as a child his reading reflected an interest in history, consisting mainly of epics and stories of great heroes. As he matured, he became acutely conscious of his own link with the past.

In point of historical fact, the path to the most powerful office on earth for John F. Kennedy had its origins in a chain of circumstances a century before in Ireland. For many generations Ireland had been a land of troubles. In 1845 and 1846 the all-important potato crops were lost to blight. This national catastrophe multiplied the misery of the people like maggots. Some families became wanderers, vainly traveling from ruined field to field in the hope of finding a crop that had been spared. Many starved and were left dying in the ditches by the side of the road while others remained in their small homes, clinging to the hope of a miracle that never came. To starvation was added the curse of typhus, and thousands more perished.

But some Irishmen had a vision—a dream of leaving the scourged land and making their way to the golden haven across the sea—America. By selling or pawning their entire belongings, some managed to scrape together the twenty pounds needed to buy a crowded steerage passage to the United States.

One of these dreamers was a youth named Patrick Kennedy. On a morning in 1850, he left his thatched-roof hut in New Ross, a town in southeast Ireland just across the river Barrow from county Kilkenny, and made his way to the sea. After paying out every last penny for his steerage ticket he boarded a Cunard Line vessel and settled down in the jammed quarters with other emigrants to endure an uncomfortable storm-tossed journey to the land of opportunity.

At last the ship docked at a place called Noddle's Island, in the crowded harbor of East Boston, Massachusetts. Strong and ambitious, Patrick Kennedy immediately found work in a cooperage, making barrels. Together with thousands of other Irish immigrants he settled in a crowded corner of East Boston, where life was hard and the families of the workingmen were crammed together in cellars, lofts and dingy tenements. Despised by the so-called "proper Bostonians" because of their poverty and Roman Catholicism, the new arrivals were objects of intense prejudice and discrimination.

As a result, the Irish in Boston became a close-knit, clannish group, clinging together for mutual solace and protection. In the shantytowns of East Boston they married, gave birth, raised their children and died. It was a pattern repeated in New York City, Chicago and other large cities where the Irish settled.

Pat Kennedy managed to get along. He took an Irish girl as his wife, and they had three daughters and a son. Then, just before the outbreak of the Civil War, he died, leaving his widow with a family to support. Mrs. Kennedy went to work in a shop while the girls looked after Patrick J., the youngest. After attending a Roman Catholic parochial school, little Pat went to work on the docks to help support his mother and sisters. Then one day when he was about eighteen he noticed that although the laborers worked hard for their wage, they invariably spent some of it in the saloon across the street from the piers as soon as the workday was over. It gave him an idea. By scrimping and borrowing, he managed to collect enough money to set himself up in the saloon business in a favorable location opposite a shipyard.

Within a few years the single establishment had expanded to a chain of saloons. Patrick Kennedy also bought an interest in a coal company and in various other enterprises. He decided to enter politics, for it was one of the few ways by which a Boston Irishman could make a reputation and achieve status for himself and his family. Soft-spoken and reserved—austere even—Patrick carried himself with an impressive air and soon became a power in Democratic ward politics. He served terms as fire commissioner, street commissioner and election commissioner. He married Mary Hickey, a girl from one of the most respected Irish families in Boston. In 1888, Mary gave birth to a son, Joseph Patrick. By this time, the Kennedys had definitely achieved "lace curtain" status as contrasted to Patrick's "shanty Irish" origins.

While Patrick Kennedy was busy making a success of himself, a similar course was being pursued by a youth named John F. Fitzgerald. Like Kennedy, young Fitzgerald had been on his own since childhood. Orphaned at sixteen, he had worked hard to support the younger members of his family.

A short, personable man with a keen wit and an

amazing gift for making friends, he had talked his way into a clerkship in the customhouse. Then he started running for political office—as councilman, alderman, state legislator, United States Congressman and, lastly, Mayor of Boston.

It had been a steady, determined rise, and in the process bouncy John Fitzgerald—or "Honey Fitz" as he was popularly known—had become one of Boston's most beloved political figures. He was a genius at the art of political showmanship and prided himself on having mastered a technique known as the "Irish switch" which consisted of engaging the attention of two voters at the same time. Indeed, Honey Fitz improved on it. While shaking the hand of one constituent and conversing with a second, he managed to gaze fondly at a third, giving each one the impression that he was the sole object of attention!

John Fitzgerald married Josephine Mary Hannon, the daughter of a prominent Irish family in nearby Lexington. The couple had a daughter, Rose, who became the light of Honey Fitz's life.

Since the Kennedys and Fitzgeralds were both involved in Democratic politics in Boston, they knew each other and sometimes found themselves working together as allies. But the plain truth was that taciturn Patrick did not like Honey Fitz because he was too outgoing and boisterous. And for his part, the little man regarded Patrick Kennedy as dry, humorless and antisocial.

Therefore, it was a minor blow to both families to learn that Joe Kennedy was courting lovely Rose Fitzgerald. Despite opposition from both sides, the young couple declared their intention of getting married.

Actually, most parents would have considered the

Kennedy boy a perfect husband for a daughter. He came from a well-off, socially acceptable family; he was handsome and athletic; he was hard-working and ambitious.

At the age of nine, young Joe had been a candy butcher on the Boston excursion boats. Then he got a job as an office boy in a bank. After attending parochial school and the famous Boston Latin School he enrolled at Harvard, but he continued to work hard at earning money. During the summers he played semiprofessional baseball and ran a sightseeing bus. Although his academic grades were mediocre, he was a top college athlete and was recognized as one of the most gifted business brains in the student body. As a result he was recruited by several undergraduate organizations, generally winding up as finance chairman.

Joe Kennedy's biggest disappointment at Harvard was being turned down by some of the elite student clubs because he was Irish and a Catholic. So he channeled his resentment into a redoubled effort to make money, convinced that great wealth was one way to achieve independence and respect, if not acceptance. By the time he was graduated from college he had a stake of five thousand dollars from his various summer enterprises. To Rose Fitzgerald he promised that this was just the beginning; she listened in awe as this remarkable young man vowed that he would have a million dollars by the time he was thirty-five!

After graduation, Joe decided to go into banking. Through Patrick Kennedy's political influence, he obtained a fifteen-hundred-a-year job as a state bank examiner. He had studied the theory of banking in some of his college courses, and he now wanted to learn the practical side of the business. One day, he heard that the Columbia Trust Company was about to be absorbed by a competing savings bank. This was big news, for Columbia Trust was a neighborhood institution catering almost exclusively to the East Boston Irish community; in fact, his own father was one of the stockholders! Sensing its importance to those families, Joe Kennedy was convinced it could become a profitable enterprise.

He persuaded cautious Patrick Kennedy and a number of relatives and friends to pool whatever cash they could raise and turn it over to him for the purpose of gaining control of the bank. With this investment fund he bought a large block of stock and personally visited dozens of stockholders to obtain their voting proxies. Before the bank officers knew what was happening, Joseph P. Kennedy had managed to wrest control of the company and have himself elected president. He was then twenty-five!

Even John Fitzgerald now had to admit that the young man who was courting his daughter Rose knew his way with a dollar. He withdrew his objections to their betrothal. On October 7, 1914, Rose Fitzgerald and Joe Kennedy were married in the private chapel of the Archbishop of Boston.

The youthful Kennedys returned from their honeymoon and settled down in a rambling house in a lower middle class section of Brookline, a suburb of Boston. Within a short time young Kennedy showed that his uncanny gift for making money was no flash in the pan. Under his management, the Columbia Bank began to show a tidy profit.

While Joe earnestly dedicated himself to the task of fulfilling his pledge to be a millionaire by the time he was thirty-five, Rose Kennedy was busy producing a family. Within a year of their marriage, she gave birth to a son, Joseph, Jr. Less than two years later, on May 29, 1917, she gave birth to a second son. They named him John Fitzgerald Kennedy, after his maternal grandfather.

By this time, America was at war with Germany. With the country desperately in need of merchant ships, Joe Kennedy turned over the management of the bank to his father to accept a position as assistant general manager of Bethlehem Steel's massive shipyards in Quincy, Massachusetts. He applied his shrewd business sense to putting the operation on a more efficient footing by setting up a cafeteria on company property so the men wouldn't have to waste time leaving the yard for meals. Not only did this increase production, but the food service also earned a profit for the company!

In spite of his success in shipbuilding Joe Kennedy had no intention of making it his life's work. He was primarily interested in high finance—for that was where the money was. The job with Bethlehem had given him a chance to study big business operations at close range, and by 1918, with World War I over, he was ready to move on.

As a result of his own experience in the shipbuilding industry, he managed to obtain an interview with Galen Stone, a Wall Street investment tycoon who also controlled a big shipping line. Stone was so impressed by the ambition, personality and financial astuteness of this young man that he hired him as head of the stock department of his investment firm, Hayden, Stone.

Joe Kennedy was off and running.

For the next five years he studied Wall Street from

the inside out. At the same time he began to speculate boldly in stocks. He bought into companies—including some in the fast-growing motion-picture industry —reshuffled them and sold out at a huge profit. He took over a chain of motion-picture theatres, shared in highly profitable investment pools and began to accumulate huge sums of money. By 1924 he was so involved in his personal deals that he left Hayden, Stone to be free to operate entirely on his own. He soon gained a reputation as one of the biggest stock speculators in the country. In 1923, by the time he was thirty-five, Joe Kennedy could boast that he had fulfilled his vow to make a million dollars several times over.

As the Kennedy fortune grew, so did the Kennedy family. During the 1920's Rose Kennedy gave birth to five daughters—Rosemary, Kathleen, Eunice, Patricia and Jean. Then came two more sons, Robert F. and the baby of the family, Edward. In all, there were nine Kennedy children, four sons and five daughters.

By now, Joseph Kennedy was an intimate of the leaders in business, government and entertainment. A lifelong Democrat who had been weaned on politics, he vigorously backed the liberal wing of the Democratic party. In 1924 he supported the Progressive ticket—a third party—which was running the famous Wisconsin Senator Robert M. La Follette as its presidential candidate. In spite of his own wealth, Kennedy felt that the common people were in desperate need of the social reforms promised by the Progressives. But La Follette lost.

In 1929 America suddenly found itself in the stranglehold of a major depression. Joe Kennedy's business acumen, combined with a mystical instinct, had led him to sell out his stock holdings before the great Wall Street crash. As a result, he found himself richer than before, since the value of cash had risen and most of his assets were now in cash reserves.

But most of the country was not so fortunate. Some businessmen lost everything. Jobless workers sold apples on street corners to earn a few cents with which to feed their families. A deadly pall of defeat and despair blanketed every corner of America.

In this atmosphere of national disillusionment and misery Joseph P. Kennedy decided in 1932 to back the presidential candidacy of an old friend and Democrat, Franklin Delano Roosevelt, against the incumbent, Herbert Hoover, a Republican. It was a decision that was to have profound consequences on the entire Kennedy family, and particularly on the life of John F. Kennedy, his second oldest son, whom they all called "Jack."

Jack Kennedy's earliest memory was of the large sprawling house on Beals Street in Brookline. It was a house forever buzzing with activity, for his father was constantly pursued by telegrams and phone calls from distant places. Invariably there were swarms of visitors —business aides, financiers, politicians. As Jack grew older and his father became more important in the world of high finance, the telegrams and long-distance calls increased and the visitors were even more numerous. Within the Kennedy family, even at the dinner table, politics was a constant source of discussion, and as the children grew up, they were encouraged to participate.

With his financial interests scattered all over the country, Joseph Kennedy was often away from Boston for days or even weeks at a time. But when he was home he tried to spend every available moment with his wife and children. Yet he could never divorce himself entirely from business matters, and his tendency toward preoccupation became a family joke. Once, when Joe, Jr. was small, his father decided to pull him around the snowy streets of Brookline on a sled. So engrossed was the elder Kennedy in planning a business deal that he did not notice that his son had toppled off. The child was found later, playing happily in a snowbank.

As the children grew older, Joseph Kennedy plunged into their activities with all the exuberance that he normally displayed in a Wall Street speculation. He participated with them in swimming, softball, tennis, sailing and golf. Family contests were encouraged, for the elder Kennedy had a simple theory: if his children were forced to compete among themselves they would be better prepared to accept a world that could be harsh, even cruel. Still embittered and resentful at the discrimination he had encountered, he was fiercely determined to expose his children to reality at the earliest possible age.

Encouraged by their father, the Kennedy youngsters contested savagely. In tennis or touch football, in swimming or boating, the emphasis was on outdoing each other. The girls would compete with the boys with no quarter asked or given. Mr. Kennedy was fond of telling his children that anyone who wasn't concerned with winning wasn't worth much. The admonition was effective.

Yet in spite of the fierce intrafamily rivalry, the Kennedys were held together by bonds of loyalty and devotion to each other that amazed everyone with whom they came in contact. It was the traditional cohesiveness of the East Boston Irish, carried to an extreme.

In truth, the steadying influence in the family was Rose Kennedy. She was the opposite of her intense, hard-driving, hot-tempered husband. Gentle, self-contained, reserved, she kept the Kennedy household on an even keel. Extremely pious, she encouraged her children to attend church regularly and to concern themselves with their spiritual needs. Bound by a deep sense of devotion and duty, she fulfilled her husband's role on numerous occasions, when he was away from home, by taking the children to museums, to places of historical interest or on visits to relatives. Gifted with a magnificent instinct for organization, Mrs. Kennedy kept records on her numerous children—cards that contained such information as dates of vaccination, illnesses and special health problems!

Despite the difficulty of raising nine active youngsters, she managed to devote some time to each of them individually—listening to their special problems, giving advice and encouraging them to make the most of their opportunities and talents. Often, when the weather was bad and there was little to occupy the children, she would organize discussions and current events games, in an effort to encourage them to keep up with what was happening in the world.

In later years Jack Kennedy was to recall his mother as perennially youthful and attractive. Moreover, she was possessed of a quiet inner courage which enabled her to cope with personal tragedy that doubtless would have broken a lesser spirit. It was a quality she managed to instill in all her children.

The first major test of Rose Kennedy's spiritual equilibrium came with the birth of her first daughter, Rosemary. A quiet, sweet child, she showed early tendencies of being withdrawn and unable to cope with the rough-and-tumble activities which her father encouraged among the other children. Rosemary was taken to a series of doctors and special clinics, but by the time she reached school age it was tragically clear that she was mentally retarded. Instead of resigning herself to despair or self-pity, Mrs. Kennedy immediately went to work developing a regimen of special activities and instruction for the little girl. Her avowed purpose was to enable her daughter to become as self-reliant as possible within the limits of her mental capacity. Wherever possible, too, Rosemary was included in family activities, and her brothers and sisters were encouraged to treat her with kindness and understanding, not pity. In this way, Rose Kennedy managed to minimize the tragic consequences which her daughter's condition might otherwise have had on the rest of the family.

Perhaps because of Rosemary's handicap, Mr. and Mrs. Kennedy were even more acutely concerned than most parents with the intellectual development of their other children. The first school attended by Jack was the Dexter School, a private academy in Brookline. His brother Joe was also a pupil there. Though he did his lessons dutifully, Jack was not particularly fond of the restrictive atmosphere of the classroom. Furthermore, Joe, who was two years ahead of him, was a fine student who brought home excellent grades. Invariably, Mr. Kennedy used his oldest son's achievements as the standard for Jack to follow.

When Jack's marks were below average, his father accusingly reminded him that his older brother was outpacing him. Here, however, the elder Kennedy's attempt to encourage healthy rivalry and competition between his two oldest sons seemed to have the reverse effect. Instead of spurring Jack to greater effort, it dulled his taste for academic pursuits and left him frustrated and depressed, for Jack was essentially a quiet, shy boy who disliked seeing his father upset or angry.

To Jack, the most agreeable aspect of going to school was the pleasure of looking forward to weekends, holidays and vacations, for at those times he did not run the risk of incurring his father's displeasure at his academic deficiencies. Besides, there were many pleasant things to do. Sometimes Grandpa Fitz would come by and take the boys to a baseball game or to the Public Garden to ride in the boats. On other occasions, they visited Plymouth Rock, Concord Bridge or some of the other famous historical landmarks in and around Boston. But just before Election Day was the most exciting time of all. Honey Fitz, still active in politics, toured the wards with his two small grandsons in tow, introducing them to some of his old friends and political cronies, colorful characters all, who entertained the boys in thick Irish brogues.

Sometimes, Joseph Kennedy crowded the whole family into his huge touring car and drove them over to old Patrick Kennedy's house. However, Grandfather Kennedy was sterner and less outgoing than lively Grandpa Fitz. On Sundays the children were forbidden to cut up in his house, and any loud or boisterous talk would draw a look of sharp rebuke from him.

By the mid-1920's Joseph Kennedy had outgrown Boston and decided to move his family to New York. He was now so heavily involved in Wall Street activities that it had become all but impossible to run his affairs from Boston. Mrs. Kennedy was not at all in favor of moving. She felt that it was unfair to the children to disrupt their schooling, their friendships and the routine of family life. However, her husband argued that there was no alternative. Actually, he had no compunction about leaving his native city, for it held bitter associations for him. In spite of his great wealth and important political connections, he had never been able to penetrate the wall surrounding the Back Bay Boston aristocracy. "My daughters would never be able to join their debutante clubs," he observed with rancor.

It also irritated him to have the Boston newspapers refer to him as an Irishman. "I was born here, and my children were born here," he noted. "What do I have to do to be an American?"

The Kennedys settled in a large house in Riverdale, a suburbanlike corner of the Bronx, within easy commuting distance of downtown Manhattan. But even that house wasn't large enough for the whole family, so a short time later, the Kennedys took title to an eleven-bedroom home in nearby Bronxville, a fashionable section in Westchester County.

Jack was registered at the nearby Riverdale School, a private institution. Here, he did his work quietly if in undistinguished fashion. Joe's scholastic triumphs continued to mount, so that the specter of failure—of being admonished by his father as an "also-ran"—again haunted Jack.

In spite of his school difficulties, he was an avid reader, and was rarely without a book. He loved stories of adventure, especially those that told of the early days of English history, and his imagination was peopled with knights and kings who lived in the age of chivalry.

A small, slight youngster, Jack was subject to frequent colds and other illnesses. Once, when he was in bed, he happened to read Sir Walter Scott's *Ivanhoe,* and it immediately became one of his favorite books. In the mind of Jack Kennedy, world history was thus transformed into the story of larger-than-life heroes resplendent in gleaming suits of armor astride snowy white steeds. If it was a child's unreal view, it was nevertheless a pleasant escape from humdrum subjects like arithmetic and spelling—particularly spelling, for Jack was a notoriously poor speller.

At thirteen he completed the sixth grade at Riverdale School and was ready to go on to more advanced work. After some thought, Joseph Kennedy, at the urging of his wife, agreed to send Jack to the Canterbury School, a Roman Catholic institution, in New Milford, Connecticut. Although Mr. Kennedy was convinced it would be better to have his son attend a secular school so he could meet boys of other religious backgrounds, his wife felt that Jack should have some Roman Catholic training. She pointed out that since he had not been exposed to religious teaching at the Riverdale School, it would be well to enroll him now in a place where he would be taught some theology. Mr. Kennedy finally relented.

Jack's first weeks at Canterbury were a time of painful adjustment. He had never been away from the family before, and he suffered agonizing spells of homesickness. However, once he was settled in the routine of the school, he threw himself into its activities with zest. An important reason was his separation from Joe, who was attending Choate, a select private school with strong Episcopal roots. No longer faced with the prospect of measuring up to his older brother, he was much more at ease with others and with himself.

He tried out for football, baseball and several other

school sports and reported home proudly that he could swim fifty yards in thirty seconds. He also joined the Boy Scouts. Even his intellectual horizons were broadening—he wrote to his father for a subscription to the *Literary Digest* magazine or a newspaper, so he would know what was going on in the world.

By the second half of the school year Jack had begun to develop close ties of loyalty to Canterbury. He liked the school and was on his way to making many new friends. But just before the Easter holidays, he fell ill. The school physician diagnosed it as appendicitis and advised that he be taken home immediately.

He was rushed to Bronxville and brought to a hospital where an operation was performed for the removal of his appendix. He never returned to Canterbury.

3

PREP SCHOOL DAYS

During his son's convalescence, Joseph Kennedy began to have second thoughts about Jack's schooling. Although he had originally agreed that the boy should be enrolled at a Roman Catholic institution, the more he thought about it, the more convinced he was that his first instinct had been right. Jack *ought* to attend a secular school, like Joe.

He reopened the issue with his wife, who was convinced that Jack should return to Canterbury. But Joseph Kennedy could be stubborn and persuasive when he wanted to, and in this instance he was both. It was finally decided that the boy would go to Choate in the fall. In return for this concession, he agreed to permit the girls to attend parochial schools. Jack himself would have preferred to return to Canterbury; yet he knew how strong-willed his father could be, so he did not even bother to enter a protest.

Choate was located on a quiet, tree-shaded campus at Wallingford, Connecticut. It was considered an extremely exclusive prep school. Some of the wealthiest and most influential families in America sent their sons there. Founded in 1896, it had a student body of five hundred and fifty young men, whose ages ranged from

24

twelve to seventeen. Although headed by an Episcopal clergyman and rooted in Anglican influence, the school was run strictly along nondenominational lines. Every boy was required to attend daily chapel as well as religious services in his own particular faith. There was also a work program: each student was assigned for at least half an hour a day to tasks like gardening, cleaning up student quarters or waiting on tables in the dining hall.

Jack Kennedy came to Choate in the fall in a gloomy frame of mind. He felt he had one large strike against him—the presence on the campus of his brother Joe. Tall, handsome and athletic like their father, Joe had already established an enviable record for scholarship and sports.

Jack knew that achievements like Joe's were hard to equal let alone beat. Having been bested by his brother in so many things in the past, he was not happy at the prospect of being forced by their father to compete against Joe again.

Yet, in spite of his sense of inadequacy, it never once occurred to him to give up without a struggle. Though small and frail he doggedly tried out for half a dozen sports, including football, baseball, basketball and swimming. He failed to make even a single varsity team.

In his studies, the record was equally dismal. Despite a sincere attempt to apply himself, he was in deep trouble over Latin. At one point his marks in this subject were ten points below the passing grade.

Torn between a deep need to succeed and a sense of frustration, Jack decided to make a desperate effort. All right, if he didn't qualify for the varsity he would play intramural sports. And he did, with determination and drive if not with grace and style. He even knuckled down sufficiently in his studies to get some good grades, and on such occasions his father rewarded him liberally. Once it was a pony, another time a sailboat. Nevertheless, it was the feeling of accomplishment itself that gave Jack the most joy, for it was a satisfaction he did not experience too often.

These were Jack Kennedy's growing-up years, and in many ways his perspective on life was beginning to change. Physically, he was growing rapidly and his voice was getting deeper, so that his sense of manliness was enhanced. He even found himself interested in girls for the first time. Attendance at dancing class was required at Choate, but Jack had been a reluctant student. Now he found himself looking forward eagerly to improving his dancing ability. He never missed an opportunity to escort a young lady to one of the school proms.

Although school was an important focal point for the two oldest Kennedy boys, there were frequent weekends and holidays when Jack and Joe returned to Bronxville to spend time with the family. In addition to their Westchester home, the Kennedys now owned a house in Palm Beach, Florida, where everybody gathered for the Christmas holidays, and a seventeen-room summer home in Hyannis Port, Massachusetts, a picture postcard resort on the shore of Nantucket Sound.

It was at Hyannis Port that Jack developed an affection for the sea. He enjoyed tennis, golf and other sports, but he loved the water most of all. He soon developed into a superb swimmer and an excellent sailor. His father had given him his own sailboat as a reward for achieving fair grades in school, and he named the boat *Victura,* under the mistaken impression that it meant "Victory" in Latin. He and Joe were active members of the Hyannis Port Yacht Club, and together they often represented Hyannis Port in sailing races against neighboring clubs.

In spite of occasional instances of cooperation between the two youths and the solid front of Kennedy unity displayed to the outside world, Joe and Jack's relationship with each other remained essentially one of fierce competition and even antagonism.

Not only was Joe more handsome, popular and athletic than Jack, not only did he earn better grades, but as the oldest child in the family he was given considerable authority over the others. Rose Kennedy, with her keen sense of family organization, saw that the simple technique of delegating responsibility to the oldest in a large household could make life a lot easier for the parents. Accordingly, when she and her husband were away from home, the first-born son was placed in charge of the rest.

Like most youngsters, Joe often took advantage of the authority given him! He behaved like a youthful tyrant, often enforcing his orders with his fists.

Jack resented this conspicuous display of authority. He was convinced that it was his duty as the next oldest to protect the younger children from Joe's bullying. So there were frequent fist fights. Sometimes the battles were fought throughout the length of the huge Kennedy home. The shouting and the sounds of scuffling were so frightening to the younger children that they invariably scampered upstairs to cower or hide until servants raced in and separated the two combatants. Because Jack was smaller, lighter and less muscular than Joe he invariably got the worst of these fights.

Except for frequent disputes between the two oldest boys, the Kennedy children had an amazing affection for one another. Because of her handicap, Rosemary was treated with tenderness and consideration by all. But it was Kathleen—nicknamed "Kick"—a lively, lovable tomboy, who was Jack's favorite. As the second oldest daughter she was close to him in age. She loved sports and games and usually held her own with the boys. It was Kick to whom he turned when he needed someone to confide in or to give him solace when he was moody or unhappy.

Aside from members of his family, there were not many people with whom Jack could develop an easy or familiar relationship, for he was not nearly as outgoing as his older brother. His best friend was a fellow Choate student, LeMoyne Billings, the scion of a wealthy Baltimore family. Like Jack, "Les" Billings was a quiet and unspectacular student who was often in academic hot water. And perhaps because of their mutual problems, they were drawn to each other.

After Joe was graduated from Choate, he enrolled at his father's Alma Mater, Harvard. Life for Jack became a little easier as the sense of sharp rivalry diminished somewhat with his brother's departure. Yet it had little effect on his marks, for he was now plagued with the complex anxieties of growing up. Jack was too concerned with his inability to excel in sports and the need to improve his popularity to give much thought to intellectual pursuits.

Yet while young Jack Kennedy was wrestling with the intensely personal problems of postadolescence, America and the rest of the world were having difficulties, too. The global depression that had begun in 1929 was making itself felt in all areas of human activity.

Unemployment and poverty were rampant in this country and abroad, bringing twin scourges of hunger and despair. Coupled with the economic crisis were disillusionment and instability in international affairs.

In the Far East, Japan, a virtual military dictatorship, had seized Manchuria from China and turned it into a puppet Japanese state. But there was no effective action by the League of Nations which had been established to discourage such aggression. The pages of daily newspapers told of the rise to power in Germany of a new ultranationalist political party known as the National Socialists, or Nazis, headed by Adolf Hitler, a funny-looking Austrian with a Charlie Chaplin mustache. In Italy, a would-be Caesar named Benito Mussolini had seized control of the government years before and was boasting that he would expand his nation's boundaries to coincide with those of the old Roman empire.

In America, however, the people joined together to solve their problems in a manner that reflected their democratic heritage. In 1932, they elected Franklin Delano Roosevelt as President of the United States.

Although Roosevelt came from a wealthy family, he understood that the people needed relief from economic despair if they were to retain faith in themselves and in democracy. Accordingly, he advocated progressive measures to help the jobless and give the nation a "new deal."

Joseph Kennedy had been impressed by Roosevelt from the start. He contributed money to his campaign and gave him strong political support. Soon they became close personal friends.

On taking office in March of 1933, the new President immediately introduced many measures to revive the economy and protect the people against further stock market collapses like the one which had triggered the debacle of 1929. One of these laws was the Securities and Exchange Act which set up a Securities and Exchange Commission as a regulatory agency. Its task was to protect the public by eliminating shady and fraudulent practices in the stock market. To the surprise of many, Roosevelt's choice for the chairman of this new watchdog commission was Joseph P. Kennedy. Some of the new President's own supporters expressed shock and dismay, for Kennedy was known as one of the nation's leading stock speculators. To ask such a man to clean up Wall Street, they charged bitterly, was like asking a wolf to protect a herd of sheep.

In spite of these protests, Roosevelt stood his ground and refused to give in to the anti-Kennedy pressure. It was soon clear that those who had opposed Kennedy's appointment were wrong. As a stock market "insider" himself he knew all the tricks and crooked schemes used by unscrupulous stock promoters to fleece the public. He went after these brokers with such a vengeance that at the end of the first fifteen months of the Security and Exchange Commission's existence it had won the respect of the entire nation.

Having placed the new agency on a sound footing, Joseph Kennedy decided to return to the financial world. For a short time he served as a highly paid consultant for the Radio Corporation of America and Paramount Pictures. But having once sampled the satisfactions of public service, he was no longer content to remain in private business. Moreover, having earned an immense fortune—some estimated it as between $50,000,000 and $100,000,000!—he felt a keen sense of obligation to repay the nation that had made his success possible.

Therefore he gave his time to Roosevelt on a voluntary basis, serving as a confidant and companion. FDR enjoyed the razor-sharp mind and penetrating wit of this tall, youthful-looking financial wizard. Often he would solicit Kennedy's advice on important economic matters before making a decision.

As a result of their close association with the President of the United States, the Kennedys soon became one of the most famous families in America. The fact that there were nine Kennedy children merely whetted the public's curiosity about this interesting Irish-American clan, and the newspapers ran items about the Kennedys almost daily.

Characteristically, Rose Kennedy did her best to keep fortune and fame from spoiling her children. The girls were sent to parochial schools, and school officials were instructed to treat them exactly like the rest of the pupils.

However, for Jack there were new personal problems. Because he was the son of Joseph P. Kennedy, he felt that people demanded more of him. He imagined that they expected him to be more courteous, more athletic, more witty and more intelligent than others his age. No matter how hard he tried it seemed to him that his accomplishments were not enough to make the grade. He had a desperate yearning to succeed, to be the best at something. Fate, however, seemed to decree otherwise. It seemed as if Jack Kennedy, unlike his brother Joe, was destined to a life of mediocrity, doomed to be the black sheep of the Kennedy family.

In the spring of 1935 he sat down with his friend Les Billings and together they discussed their college plans. Billings was scheduled to go to Princeton, just as it had always been assumed that Jack would follow the Kennedy family tradition and enroll at Harvard. In the course of their conversation the two boys speculated on how pleasant it would be if they could both matriculate at the same university and remain friends and roommates.

The more they discussed the possibility, the more enthusiastic they became. Les urged his friend to write to his parents and ask for permission to enroll at Princeton. Jack finally agreed it was worth a try, even at the risk of horrifying his father, a loyal Harvard alumnus.

To Jack Kennedy the justification for attending Princeton seemed simple enough—it would enable him to be with his best friend Les Billings. But perhaps there was another factor, one which Jack refused to admit to himself: a deep-seated desire to destroy the pattern of competition with his older brother who was attending Harvard.

To Jack's surprise, his father did not raise strenuous objections to his plan. If that was what he wanted, Joseph Kennedy told his son, he could have his wish and enroll at Princeton. He trusted, of course, that Jack had given the matter considerable thought and had examined the advantages and disadvantages carefully. After all, Harvard was a fine university and there was a certain amount of family tradition associated with attendance there. . . .

Jack assured his father that he was certain about wanting to attend Princeton. In late spring he and Les Billings filed their applications to enroll as freshmen in the fall.

Jack was so delighted at receiving his father's approval that he did not even mind it when the elder

Kennedy suggested he spend the summer doing academic spadework for his college courses. Jack was honest enough to admit that his scholastic record at Choate had been nothing to cheer about. Perhaps some preliminary studying would be a good thing, he told himself. He was even more amenable to the plan when his father offered to send him to England for the summer to attend the London School of Economics under the distinguished Socialist professor, Harold J. Laski.

Mr. Kennedy had met Laski years before in Boston. He was immediately impressed with the man's genius, even though they did not necessarily agree on all political matters. Joe had studied under Laski for a summer and had been awed by the English political scientist's brilliance. Mr. Kennedy was convinced that exposure to Laski's mind and to the many-faceted cosmopolitan life of London would broaden Jack's intellectual horizons and better prepare him for college.

Jack arrived in London in July, 1935. But he had barely met Laski and started attending classes when he fell ill. His skin and the whites of his eyes turned yellow and he began to suffer attacks of nausea and itching. He visited a London physician who diagnosed the condition as jaundice and ordered him to drop all activities at once.

He returned home to the United States, where the family doctor prescribed hot baths and plenty of rest. It was weeks before Jack's skin began to clear up. By the time he was permitted to resume normal activities, classes at Princeton were well into the fall semester. Nevertheless, he registered late and received a warm welcome from Les Billings who introduced him to the other freshmen and helped him review the work he had missed.

By the time the Christmas holidays arrived, Jack was beginning to feel a part of college life. Then a recurrent attack of jaundice sent him to bed for a second time. The family physician promptly ordered him to take the rest of the academic year off. Under no circumstances was he to return to Princeton for the spring semester, the doctor warned his parents. Jack protested but Rose and Joe Kennedy announced that the prescription was to be followed scrupulously. For the rest of the school year he remained at home, reading books of biography and history.

Since it was 1936 and a presidential election was in the offing, his father was once more deeply involved in political activities on behalf of President Roosevelt. An even more vigorously outspoken "New Dealer" now than during FDR's first campaign in 1932, Mr. Kennedy took time out to write a book which he entitled *I'm for Roosevelt*. In it, he described the President's philosophy of government, politics and economics and explained why he felt it was vital for the future of the country that FDR's ideas be carried out.

Occasionally the elder Kennedy tried to discuss the campaign with Jack, but the youth was not very interested. Of course, he favored Roosevelt over the Republican nominee, Alfred Landon of Kansas, but he had no real concern with domestic politics. Nor did he feel any involvement in world affairs, although across the earth violent winds of change were blowing.

In Germany, Adolf Hitler had adopted a policy of brutal aggression to reclaim territories lost to Germany after World War I. He also instituted vicious anti-Semitic laws against German Jews. Benito Mussolini, eager to build an Italian Empire, had invaded the independent African kingdom of Ethiopia with planes and well-armed troops. In the course of the fighting, a native Ethiopian army equipped largely with spears and swords was brutally decimated. Yet not a single nation nor the League of Nations stepped in to take action against the Nazi and Fascist aggressors.

Like many others, Jack Kennedy was not aware that a harvest of future tragedy was being sown by the apathy of the Western democracies at this crucial time in history. As he recuperated from his siege of jaundice during the spring of 1936, his most immediate concern was to return to college in the fall.

Since Les Billings would be a sophomore when he enrolled as a freshman in September, Jack's original reason for going to Princeton seemed pointless. His father did not overlook this point. Under the circumstances, would it not be wise to reconsider and go to Harvard? he asked.

Jack thought seriously about his father's proposal. He could not help noting the strange similarity between the present situation and that of five years earlier during his first year at Canterbury. Then, too, he had been taken ill and had finally transferred to Choate, as the elder Kennedy had wished. It almost seemed as if some mysterious pattern of fate was operating to determine his academic destiny, not to mention his father's powers of persuasion. So in September of 1936 Jack Kennedy went up to Cambridge, Massachusetts, just outside of Boston, to enroll as a freshman at his father's Alma Mater.

4

THE SPARK IS STRUCK

Jack was only eight when the Kennedy family had left Boston a decade earlier, but for him the city held a wealth of childhood memories. After all, he had been born there, as had his parents before him and their parents before them. In fact, while old Patrick Kennedy had died in 1929, Grandpa Fitz was still alive and still very active in Boston politics.

Harvard, located in Cambridge, a suburb of Boston, was another old familiar friend. As a child, Jack had visited Harvard Yard often, and he had heard so much about the university from his father that he had always felt a certain kinship with it, in spite of his decision of the previous year to break with family tradition.

As a Harvard freshman, Jack's initial experience proved to be almost a repetition of his first year at Choate. Once again he discovered that Joe had left a record which would be hard to match, but which he, as a Kennedy, would be expected to follow.

Joe was playing varsity football and was taking honors in his studies. Moreover, gregarious and charming as always, he had run for a number of political offices on campus and won them all. There was little question that Joe Kennedy, Jr. was one of the most successful and popular students at Harvard.

Spurred on by his father, Jack tried out for football, swimming, golf and softball. Again he played with a furious energy, but his determination outpaced his skill. Even in swimming, his best sport, he encountered bad luck. Just before the trials were held to select members of the swimming team that was to compete against Yale, he came down with a severe cold and was sent to the infirmary.

Fearful that he would miss the trials, he talked a classmate into smuggling thick steaks and chocolate malted milks into the infirmary to build up his strength. Then, still suffering from fever, he dressed and sneaked off to the pool building and participated in the trials. In spite of the fact that he swam with all his might, he lost in his heat and failed to place on the team!

Misfortune dogged him on the football field, too. Although too light and untalented to make the first-string freshman team, he played as a member of the second-string, hoping to prove to the coach that he could make up in sheer grit and determination what he lacked in skill. One day, during practice, he was tackled so hard that he hurt his back. The trainer taped it up, but within the next few days the pain became so intense that he reported to the college medical office. The physician examined his back and told him that it was more than a sprain, possibly a spinal injury. He was to avoid all violent exercise or bodily contact sports until his back was completely healed. It marked the end of his college football days.

One favorable outcome of his brief football career was his friendship with Torbert Macdonald. Macdonald, a member of Jack's class, was a husky, handsome athlete who had been a football star in high school. He and Jack met while both were trying out for the team. Macdonald made the first-string freshman squad easily and was soon being mentioned for the varsity the following year.

Jack and "Torby" Macdonald became friends immediately. For Jack, who was not as outgoing as his brother Joe and thus was not favored with a wide circle of chums, it was important to have at least one or two close friends. At Choate, it had been Les Billings. Now, it was Torby Macdonald, and they became roommates.

Jack's freshman program included courses in English, French, history and economics. Except for a B in economics, he drew three C's, which placed him academically in the second lowest group of passing students in the freshman class. It was far from an auspicious start, particularly in light of Joe's record. Still, he felt a sense of relief that he had passed all his courses, for he had been told that for many students the freshman year was a difficult period of adjustment.

Aside from sports, there were many activities at Harvard for an eager student who wanted the full taste of college life. Jack ran for president of the freshman class against thirty-three other candidates and was beaten badly, whereupon he settled for the chairmanship of the committee to arrange the traditional Freshman Smoker. He joined several clubs including the St. Paul's Catholic Club and the Hasty Pudding, which put on Harvard's annual musical revue. He also applied for a berth on the Harvard *Crimson,* the undergraduate newspaper, and was given a position on the business staff.

There was one area in which Jack was completely disinterested: political activity. The campus was a cauldron of varying philosophies. There were student groups representing the entire political spectrum: Young Democrats and Young Republicans; pacifists and Socialists; thinkers and activists of almost every persuasion. Sometimes the political-minded students would debate and argue far into the night. Or they would organize picket lines in protest against the world's varied ills.

But this sort of activity was foreign to Jack Kennedy's life at Harvard. Perhaps because he had been close to it since birth, he felt an apathy toward politics and wanted no part of it. Even foreign affairs, now an important focal point of attention because of the aggressions of the Nazis and Fascists, failed to excite his concern.

As the spring of his freshman year arrived, his goal was still to make a name for himself on campus, so that no one, especially his father, could accuse him of defaulting in the competition with his brother. By the time Easter came, the heavy combination of studying and extracurricular activities left Jack exhausted. At home during the spring vacation his father proposed that he take a trip to Europe on his own during the coming summer. It was to make up in part for the curtailment of his stay in England the previous year.

The offer came with the pleasant impact of an unexpected birthday gift and he thanked his father and sat down eagerly to plan his itinerary. Then it occurred to him that it would be more exciting to travel with a good friend. He knew that Torby Macdonald's plans for the summer were already set but would Les Billings be willing to go? When he called Billings no persuasion was necessary. Les was enthusiastic, and if it was okay with his parents, they were all set.

For Jack the summer of 1937 was a voyage of discovery. He and Billings traveled through France, Spain and Italy tasting the sights and sounds of Mediterranean Europe. In Monte Carlo they sampled the gambling casinos, playing with five-franc chips. Except for his brief stay in England the previous year, Jack had never been on his own before, so the wine of freedom proved a heady experience. He and Les were free to go and do as they pleased. They talked with hitchhikers, street vendors, reporters and diplomats. Letters of introduction from his father served as magic tickets of admission everywhere. In Rome Jack had an audience with Pope Pius XI and the Pope's aide, Cardinal Pacelli, who was a personal friend of Mr. Kennedy's. They saw a bullfight, climbed Mount Vesuvius and loafed when they felt like it. Everywhere there were exciting things to see and question.

The trip was a turning point for Jack. His intellectual curiosity had been unlocked, and for the first time he began to feel an emergent concern about the world. At Harvard he had been unmoved by the frenetic student activities in politics and political philosophy. Now he suddenly felt a personal involvement, for he was *there*—at the very places where history was being made. He observed the terror spread by the Nazi and Fascist dictatorships and recognized for the first time the fear of war in people's eyes.

When Jack returned to Harvard in the fall, his newly awakened interest in government and world events was stimulated by another happening. With the election of President Franklin D. Roosevelt to a second term of office the year before, Joseph P. Kennedy's political stock had risen sharply, for he had been one of FDR's most ardent and effective supporters. It had been rumored in government circles for months that Joe Kennedy's loyalty to "The Chief" would soon be rewarded.

Toward the end of 1937, the newspapers carried headlines that Roosevelt had appointed Mr. Kennedy as Ambassador to Great Britain. The news left many persons in the political and diplomatic world—not to mention members of the Boston aristocracy—stunned. Joe Kennedy was of Irish descent—and a Roman Catholic. Appointing him as the envoy to the Court of St. James's, the most prized of all diplomatic posts, was unthinkable!

There were bitter attacks on the President. FDR was unperturbed; so was Joseph P. Kennedy, for the latter knew only that after two decades of striving to achieve wealth and status for his family and himself, he had accomplished exactly what he had started out to do. And in the process he had proved that in America it was possible for a boy from East Boston to go almost as far as his ability could carry him. Indeed, he could not help speculating that someday it might even be possible for a Roman Catholic to be elected President of the United States!

At Harvard the news of his father's appointment enhanced Jack's sense of personal concern with world affairs. Unfortunately, this newly kindled interest did not reflect itself in improved grades during his sophomore year. In spite of a conscientious effort to do sound academic work, he found it difficult to overcome the poor preparation resulting from his low grades at Choate and during his freshman year at Harvard. As a result, he had to do a lot of remedial studying.

He received four C's, a D and one B for his sophomore year, slightly worse than his freshman grades. Still, for the first time he did not feel a sense of guilt or remorse at his poor showing. He had done his best and he knew that the year had been one of solid learning and achievement. He felt that at least he was on his way to a clearly defined goal.

In sports, too, there had been a triumph of sorts. Teamed with a fellow student named Reed, Jack had won Harvard's intercollegiate sailing award, the Mac-Millan Bowl.

Earlier in the year his father and mother, now Ambassador and Mrs. Joseph P. Kennedy, had moved to England and were living in a fine, large mansion in London with the younger children. The older boys and girls remained at school in the United States. For the first time Jack felt a true sense of separation from the family. With the Kennedys geographically dispersed, he could no longer look forward to the traditional holiday reunions that had meant so much to him in the past. His personal dependence on the family was giving way to a sense of self-reliance and maturity, and marked another turning point.

With the completion of final examinations that signified the end of his sophomore year, he and his brother Joe sailed to England to spend the summer with their family. Joe had just been graduated and was planning to go to Harvard Law School in the fall. These days, the relationship between the two oldest Kennedy boys was on a much more satisfactory footing. With adulthood had come a lessening of the intensity of their childhood rivalry. The sense of competition was still there, but resentment had mellowed into understanding, and while neither would ever be close, strong bonds of mutual respect and loyalty were indeed beginning to develop.

At the American Embassy in London, Ambassador Kennedy gave a huge twenty-first birthday party in honor of Jack. At this time, too, he informed his children that he was settling separate trust funds on each of them. He explained that in this way he would be guaranteeing their financial security so that each would be free to go his own way. If they felt financially tied to their parents' apron strings, they might never have this freedom of choice.

As the summer months slipped by, the world seemed even more glittering than Jack had customarily known it to be, in spite of an air of international tension that seemed to hang over Europe. There was swimming and boating on the Riviera and huge parties to which the finest people were invited. He dated some of the prettiest girls in Europe and wrote long letters about his life abroad to Torby Macdonald and Les Billings back home. He also read a great deal and spent many hours thinking about his own future, without coming to any conclusion about a career.

His brother, encouraged by their father, had long ago decided on a political future. In fact, Mr. Kennedy had, on numerous occasions, indicated in a bantering tone that he was grooming his oldest son to become President of the United States. Jack was not so sure it was meant only in jest, for he had long ago learned that his father was fundamentally a determined, tough-minded man whose every act was purposeful. Even his jokes usually had a serious undertone.

Jack himself had very little use for politics. He regarded such activity as seamy and unpleasant and ruled it out as a career. Joe, on the other hand, seemed

to be a born politician who had shown a keen apti-
tude for the rough and tumble of politics, even as a
student.

In September of 1938 Jack returned to Harvard for
his junior year. The semester had barely gotten under
way when international events suddenly jarred him
into the realization that the secure world he had always
known was crumbling before his eyes.

The previous March, Adolf Hitler had precipitated a
political crisis in Austria and used it as an excuse to
send in his Nazi troops to annex that country. Neither
the League of Nations nor England and France, the
strongest democracies in Europe, had done anything to
stop the dictator. Encouraged by his bold success, the
Nazi leader provoked a similar crisis in Czechoslovakia and was now threatening to crush the Czechs.

Shocked into action by this last act of naked aggression, British Prime Minister Neville Chamberlain and
French Premier Edouard Daladier met with Hitler and
Mussolini, Hitler's ally, in Munich, Germany. In return
for a pledge by the Nazi leader to maintain peace and
respect Czechoslovakian independence, the leaders of
the democracies agreed, on September 21, to cede a
portion of Czechoslovakia, known as the Sudeten territory, to Germany. This was done even though the
Czechs were not permitted to participate in the negotiations!

Prime Minister Chamberlain returned to Britain
boasting that he had bought "peace in our time," but
throughout the world there was shocked disbelief at
the realization that Czechoslovakia had been sold out
in order to appease Hitler.

The news of Munich struck with stunning impact
and it seemed to Jack, back at Harvard, that the world

was teetering precariously on the edge of disaster. He could not help feeling himself part of a tense and fear-charged era, one in which the danger of holocaust was imminent. He saw more clearly than ever that the world in which he had grown up had changed—that it would never be the same again.

5

WHY ENGLAND SLEPT

During Jack's junior year, he discovered there could be real excitement in some of his studies. He learned this lesson in a course in American government, taught by Professor Arthur N. Holcombe, one of Harvard's most popular faculty members.

Like all great teachers, Dr. Holcombe had a gift for making his subject come alive. Jack began to view the theory and practice of government in a new light. Until now, his knowledge of American politics had been derived largely from his exposure to the ward activities of Grandpa Fitz and occasional discussions with his father on FDR's policies.

It was Professor Holcombe who first made him aware that politics was an integral part of American society—that it could not be separated from other facets of life. The professor pointed out that the way politics was practiced in a particular ward told a good deal about the background and problems of the people in that neighborhood.

Jack was fascinated by this new perspective on politics and government—a view he had never been shown before. During the term, each student was required to do a research paper on a particular individual in political life. Jack was assigned Bertrand Snell, a Republican politician from upstate New York who had belonged to the extreme right wing of his party. Somewhat surprised, Jack explained to Professor Holcombe that he and his family were all Democrats. The teacher nodded. "I want to see what a Massachusetts Democrat can do with a New York Republican," he retorted slyly.

Jack worked hard on the paper, spending evenings and weekends in the Harvard library checking obscure periodicals and dog-eared copies of *The Congressional Record*.

When he finally turned in the report, Professor Holcombe was delighted with it. He told Jack that it was an excellent paper and wanted to know if he planned to make politics his career. Jack said that his brother Joe was the real politician of the family; but he added that he found the study of politics and government much more rewarding than he had ever imagined.

Soon a warm friendship developed between student and teacher. Jack was such a strong admirer of Professor Holcombe that at times he found himself thinking of college teaching as a career. The course in American government marked Jack's emergence as a student. He was now developing a true love of learning and a respect for the discipline of the mind he had never felt before.

Meanwhile, a storm was brewing in London involving Jack's father. Ambassador Kennedy had contempt for the German and Italian dictatorships. He was sickened by Nazi persecution of the Jews. At the same time, he was greatly worried by the threat of war, and he was convinced that Britain and France together were no match for Germany's military might. Moreover, he was vehemently opposed to any involvement by the United States in what he considered to be essentially Europe's problem.

Now Joseph P. Kennedy had always thought of himself as a practical man. He was convinced that the only practical course was for England and France to try to get along with the Nazi and Fascist dictatorships, particularly since Hitler, having triumphed at Munich, was proceeding with plans to dominate the Danube and the Balkan countries. Surely a new war threat was developing.

As tensions grew, the Ambassador decided to speak out in terms which he hoped other "practical men" would understand. In a speech delivered before Britain's Navy League, he declared that instead of concentrating on differences in their political philosophies, the democracies and dictatorships should emphasize their common problems and try to re-establish good relations. "After all," he added, "we have to live together in the same world, whether we like it or not."

The speech drew a loud burst of criticism by those who felt that Ambassador Kennedy was blind to the true menace of totalitarianism. These critics charged him with failing to see that Hitler's ultimate goal was domination of the world.

Jack responded to the criticism of his father's Navy League speech with mixed emotions. On the one hand he respected his father and was pained to see him the object of widespread public attack; on the other hand he could not be certain of the soundness of his father's position, for he had no personal basis on which to make a judgment.

So for the next few months he watched restlessly as headlines from Europe told of growing preparations for war, and desperately yearned to go over and see for himself what was happening.

Early in 1939 he wrote his father, asking for permission to sail to Europe in the early spring for a prolonged tour. He pointed out that he had inquired of Harvard officials and was told he could get a leave of absence. His purpose was a serious one, he explained —to study at firsthand the political situation.

The Ambassador gave his assent but established a single provision—that his son should file detailed reports on conditions in each capital he visited. Jack readily agreed.

In late winter he crossed the storm-tossed Atlantic, visited briefly with his family in London and went on to Paris where he stayed with William C. Bullitt, the American Ambassador to France. From there he proceeded to Poland and then to Russia, Turkey and Palestine. After touring the Middle East he returned to the Balkan countries, stopped off at Berlin and finally wound up in Paris again. In every place he visited he found tension and fear of war.

From each country he mailed a detailed account of what he had seen and heard. To insure objectivity, he spoke to representatives of every political party in the countries visited, as well as to newspapermen, embassy representatives and other informed persons. His letters had grammatical errors and misspellings, but they were tempered, unemotional and factual in tone. His father praised him for a superb job of diplomatic reporting.

Meanwhile, international events had been warming up to explosive heat. Hitler broke his Munich pledge to Chamberlain and swallowed up the rest of Czechoslovakia. In addition, he was demanding that Poland return the city of Danzig and other territories which

Germany had lost in World War I. Prime Minister Neville Chamberlain, though angry, pledged to support Poland against any aggression.

Troops were being called up all over Europe. An atmosphere of feverish military activity seemed to blanket the continent.

Suddenly, on August 21, a shocked and bewildered world received the news that Soviet Russia and Germany, which had been at each other's throats, had agreed on a ten-year mutual nonaggression pact!

Jack returned to the American Embassy in London to find his father and the rest of the diplomatic staff gloomily apprehensive about the future. Everyone appeared to be wondering what would happen next. But no one seemed to have any answers.

Finally, on September 1, 1939, long jack-booted columns of gray-uniformed Nazi troops strutted across the border into Poland. From the skies over cities like Warsaw and Cracow, German airplanes bombed and strafed the civilian populace in an effort to create terror and panic and break down opposition.

Two days later, on September 3, Prime Minister Chamberlain appeared in the British Parliament and announced that inasmuch as the Nazis had ignored an ultimatum to vacate Poland, a state of war existed between Germany and Great Britain. The gathering storm had burst at last.

Jack remained with his parents at their country house outside London, waiting for a boat to take him back to the States. On September 4, at three o'clock in the morning, the telephone jangled noisily. It was the American Embassy in London. Ambassador Kennedy sleepily took the call. The news jarred him awake immediately. It concerned a war incident in which Americans had been involved. Just twelve hours after Great Britain's declaration of war, a British liner, *Athenia,* had been torpedoed by the Germans several hundred miles off the northwest coast of Ireland. The passengers had included more than three hundred Americans. Some of the survivors had been taken to Scotland and put up in a Glasgow hotel.

Unable to spare anyone from the regular embassy staff, the Ambassador asked Jack to go to Scotland, question the survivors and arrange for their passage back to the States. Jack was delighted to accept the responsibility, for in the excitement of the last few days, he had begun to feel like a useless and unnecessary cog.

He entrained at once for Scotland. The information his father had asked him to obtain was important, for Radio Berlin was already disputing the charge that a German submarine was responsible for the sinking, claiming that the British had scuttled the ship themselves to stir up American feeling against Germany.

Jack arrived in Glasgow and conscientiously questioned the Americans. His investigation confirmed that a Nazi submarine had been responsible for the sinking. He assured the survivors that they would be able to secure passage on an American ship, but they loudly protested that they didn't want to sail on an unarmed ocean liner. "We want a convoy! Send the American Navy here to protect us on the way home!" Jack patiently explained that an American naval convoy was out of the question, for it would be a violation of the Neutrality Act. There was much grumbling, but Jack was firm, and they sailed on an American ship.

Returning to London, he submitted a complete report of his findings to his father; then, three weeks later, he sailed for home and Harvard.

Most of his energy was now given over to his studies. His grades had improved so markedly during the last year and a half that he found himself a candidate for honors in political science! It was quite a change from his mediocre record as a freshman.

In order to win honors he was required to submit a senior thesis, and he tackled this task with determination. His advisers were Professors Bruce Hopper and Payson Wild of the political science department. After several consultations with them, Jack decided to write on "Appeasement at Munich." Because of his personal experience in Europe, both faculty members agreed that he had chosen a pertinent topic.

Jack planned to deal specifically with the reasons for Great Britain's tardy response to the threat presented by Adolf Hitler. He himself felt that much of the emotionalism and criticism directed toward Prime Minister Neville Chamberlain as the villain of the Munich appeasement episode was unjust. He felt that Chamberlain in his actions had reflected the mood of the British people, and the fault therefore rested with a populace which had failed to wake up in time to the menace of Nazism. Jack was convinced that because of the sad state of British military preparation at the time, Chamberlain had had no alternative but to appease Hitler.

This point of view reflected in many respects Ambassador Kennedy's. He, too, felt that Chamberlain had acted properly under the circumstances. Moreover, with things going badly for the democracies—Germany had by now overrun Denmark, Norway, the Netherlands—the elder Kennedy was frantically cabling Washington that the British did not have a ghost of a chance in fighting off the Nazis. He pleaded that the United States remain completely neutral.

To prepare his paper, Jack immersed himself in the book stacks of Harvard's Widener Library, eagerly searching for copies of parliamentary debates, British Foreign Office reports and back copies of English periodicals.

Although the matters of which he was writing were as urgent as the headlines in the daily newspapers, Jack was determined that his own approach should be purely intellectual and detached. While he deplored the emotionalism of the people in attacking Chamberlain's action at Munich, he also took to task so-called practitioners of "alarmism." The report, like all undergraduate scholarly efforts, was formidably anchored in a sea of complex statistics and footnotes. However, in spite of his coldly intellectual approach throughout most of the paper, there were times when he unwittingly found himself writing with a sense of deep feeling and urgency.

Citing Great Britain's lack of preparedness as an unfortunate example, Jack urged the United States to arm itself at once in order to be prepared to meet a threat similar to that faced by the other democracies.

However, on one question he studiously avoided taking sides—the issue of American intervention on behalf of Britain and France. The elder Kennedy, of course, was urging the American government to remain neutral, but Jack was not sure that his father's position was right. Still, he felt that to espouse a point of view not in total support of his father's would be disloyal, since the Ambassador was under fire from numerous critics at home and abroad. So he solved his problem by retreating from it—by refraining from going into the issue altogether.

When the honor thesis was submitted, Jack was congratulated by his faculty advisers for a superb job. Shortly afterward, the university officially announced that the paper had been accepted *summa cum laude*—with highest honors. He immediately wrote to his father telling him the good news. The Ambassador cabled congratulations, ending the message on a high note of paternal pride: TWO THINGS I ALWAYS KNEW ABOUT YOU. ONE, THAT YOU ARE SMART. TWO, THAT YOU ARE A SWELL GUY. LOVE, DAD.

In spite of his academic triumph, however, a heavy cloud of gloom shadowed the approach of Commencement Day for Jack. By June, the Nazis were smashing through French defenses and threatening Paris. In Belgium, a huge army of British had been pressed against the sea at Dunkirk, thus forcing the emergency evacuation of four hundred thousand troops under heavy German pressure. It was beginning to look as if the Western European democracies were tragically close to the defeat which Ambassador Kennedy had been predicting.

However, Harvard went ahead with its commencement plans. There was a parade in Harvard Stadium, a baseball game with Yale and the final dance at Winthrop House. And at last the solemn Commencement itself, replete with traditional pomp and pageantry. Because of the critical war situation, Ambassador Kennedy found it impossible to leave his post in London, but Mrs. Kennedy and her other children proudly sat in the audience as Jack, dressed in black cap and gown, received his degree with honors.

The enthusiastic reception of his thesis by his professors had been a pleasant surprise to Jack. Now he had an idea, and he cautiously sounded out his father by letter. The plan: to see if he could get a publisher to accept it! Since the manuscript ran about seventy-five thousand words it certainly was long enough to be published in book form.

"I thought I could work on it rewriting it and making it somewhat more complete and maybe more interesting for the average reader," he wrote his father. "As it stands now, it is not anywhere polished enough although the ideas, etc. are O.K."

The Ambassador heartily endorsed the idea and sent him a long list of criticisms and suggestions on rewriting and editing. He also put Jack in touch with an old friend, Arthur Krock, Washington columnist of *The New York Times*.

Jack worked hard to clean up the grammar, spelling and style. He eliminated the bulky footnotes and added additional data. Then he brought the manuscript to Arthur Krock who read it and suggested that he call it *Why England Slept*—a departure from the title of a work by Winston Churchill, *While England Slept*. The newspaperman also referred him to a literary agent. Another old friend of Ambassador Kennedy's, Henry Luce, head of Time, Inc., agreed to write a foreword.

While Jack was busily putting the manuscript into final shape, the newspapers carried the tragic announcement that France had fallen to the Nazi juggernaut. The book was sent to Harper's, a leading New York publishing house, but it was rejected on the grounds that the topic had been outdated by the defeat of France. Jack was disappointed, but Arthur Krock urged him to submit it to other publishers. The second publisher to receive the manuscript, Wilfred Funk,

Inc., took just the opposite view, feeling that the tragic experience of France added to the importance and relevance of *Why England Slept*.

By rushing ahead with production, the publisher managed to get it into the bookstores by the end of July. The judgment of Funk's editors was soon validated. Sales began briskly and continued to climb. By fall, more than forty thousand copies had been sold, making the volume a best seller! Moreover, in England a like number of copies were sold, bringing total sales to eighty thousand. Ambassador Kennedy, like any proud father, sent copies to his friends—including Harold Laski, Winston Churchill and the Queen!

In the meantime, the Ambassador's reputation as a leading exponent of American isolationism continued to project him as a controversial figure. He kept up his praise for the courage of Great Britain which was now being subjected to a full-scale Nazi air blitz but urged that the United States arm to the teeth while retaining her neutrality. In spite of their magnificent heroism in the "Battle of Britain," the British did not have the resources to withstand the attack for long, Mr. Kennedy warned grimly.

In the United States, the Ambassador was receiving active support from Joe, who had been named a Massachusetts delegate to the Democratic national convention in Chicago. The junior Kennedy, convinced that FDR was leading the nation into the war, was bitterly anti-Roosevelt and announced his opposition to a third term nomination for the President.

In October, the Ambassador came home from England for a talk with Mr. Roosevelt. The President listened to his complaints and ideas and proceeded to charm him right back into the Roosevelt camp. A week before the election, Mr. Kennedy took to the air and, in a speech broadcast over one hundred and fourteen radio stations, announced his support for FDR for a third term. In spite of this unexpected turn of events, Joe, Jr. continued to oppose Roosevelt.

FDR defeated his Republican opponent Wendell Willkie by almost five million votes. Immediately afterward, the Ambassador agreed to an interview with a newspaper reporter. Pressed about his views, he issued some hasty, indiscreet statements, charging that Britain was finished as a democratic country and that he planned to organize a campaign to keep America out of the war.

Even if Roosevelt had wanted to keep him on as ambassador, he could no longer do so in the face of Mr. Kennedy's criticism of Great Britain. A storm of protest broke in the American press and abroad. Joseph P. Kennedy's career as ambassador was over. He resigned soon afterward and returned to the United States with Mrs. Kennedy and the younger children.

In spite of the controversy, Jack managed to retain his detached view. He backed Roosevelt's re-election but, unlike his brother, did not participate actively in the campaign, and he continued to refrain from taking sides on the issue of intervention.

As a matter of fact, following the publication of *Why England Slept,* Jack found himself at loose ends. At twenty-three, he was the author of a best-selling book, yet he felt restless and uncertain about the future. He thought again of an academic career but decided against it for the time being, convinced that he should seek a more active pursuit. He reconsidered law and rejected it on the grounds that it would not be useful unless he intended to go into practice or into politics. In the end, he decided to attend a graduate school of business. Why not? It might prove practical someday when he would be called upon to manage his father's vast financial and business empire.

He enrolled at Stanford University, but after a few weeks decided that a business course was not for him after all. He wrote his parents that he had decided to take a trip to South America, but because of his uncertainty about his future, the trip proved a vast disappointment. He returned to the United States and rejoined his parents.

Despite his father's continued fulminations against involvement in the war, Jack saw clearly that it was just a matter of time before the United States would be forced to take sides, and by now, so did his brother Joe. In the spring of 1941, Joe announced that he intended to enlist in the Navy in June, upon the completion of his second year at Harvard Law School. His plan was to enter the naval aviation cadet program and take flying training.

Jack was curiously torn between the temptation to emulate his brother and a desire *not* to follow in Joe's footsteps. He solved the problem by seeking enlistment in the Army. Actually, he would have preferred to enter the Army Air Corps as a flying cadet, but he knew that the old back injury from his freshman football days would keep him out of aviation training. However, to his utter chagrin, the Army physicians informed him that his back condition disqualified him from *any* military service.

He consulted a specialist to find out if anything could be done for his injury and was referred to a physical therapist. The next five months were agonizing ones as he underwent a series of strenuous treatments and exercises to strengthen his back muscles.

In September he tried again to get into the armed forces. Since his earlier disqualifying medical record was on file with the Army, he went to the Navy and applied for a commission. The Navy fitness test was strenuous, but he managed to pass.

Early in the fall he was commissioned an ensign and assigned to the Intelligence branch at naval headquarters in Washington, D.C. His task was to prepare a daily news digest for top-ranking officers. Disappointed, but philosophical about his assignment, he did his work conscientiously. He felt that all things considered, he had little reason to complain.

On Sunday morning, December 7, 1941, Japanese planes sneaked out of the Pacific sky and bombed Pearl Harbor. The United States was at war. For Jack Kennedy, a moment of truth was close at hand.

6

ABOARD THE PT'S

The mood of Americans changed overnight. With their country in a struggle for survival, bickering and internal dissension gave way to unity and a sense of purpose. The war itself had made the former arguments against intervention obsolete. The United States was now an ally of Great Britain against Germany, Italy and Japan.

Russia, too, had discovered the futility of trusting Hitler. The previous June, Germany had scrapped her ten-year mutual nonaggression pact with the Soviet Union—signed just two years before—and attacked Russia without warning.

Like all patriotic Americans, Joseph P. Kennedy was now concerned with a single goal: *winning the war*. Having recovered from the initial shock of Pearl Harbor, he sent the following wire to President Roosevelt: NAME THE BATTLEFRONT. I'M YOURS TO COMMAND.

While there was no suitable battlefront for a fifty-three-year-old former ambassador with no previous training, Ensign John F. Kennedy was more favorably situated. It was sea duty he wanted, and to get it he volunteered for "PT-boat" training. These small, sleek craft, known officially as Motor Torpedo Boats, had gained fame in the Pacific for the daredevil exploits of their skippers. Depending on surprise and speed, they raced in at dangerously close range, released their torpedoes at larger ships, then scooted out again with their brittle wooden hulls skimming the sea surface like frightened gulls.

Because of his civilian experience with small boats, Jack had no trouble qualifying. The eight-week course, given at Mellville, Rhode Island, on the shore of Narragansett Bay, consisted of seamanship, navigation, engineering, torpedo-handling and gunnery. With Jack at Mellville was his old Harvard roommate, Torbert Macdonald, also an ensign. In addition, he made two other close friends—Ensign George Ross, whom everyone called "Barney," and Ensign Paul Fay. The four became inseparable companions.

Jack's grades during PT-boat training were so outstanding that he was held over as an instructor and promoted to the rank of lieutenant (jg). The promotion was fine, but he preferred combat duty and applied for reassignment. Meantime, he saw a good deal of his family, for Hyannis Port was only fifty miles from Mellville. Joe, now an ensign, proudly wore the gold wings of a Navy pilot. Sister Kathleen—Kick—was in love with a young British nobleman, the Marquess of Hartington, whom she had met in England while her father was ambassador, and there was serious talk of marriage. Little Robert, who idolized his older brother Jack, was no longer so little. Now sixteen, "Bobby" was a student at Milton Academy in Massachusetts.

Understandably, life for the Kennedys was no longer the secure, boisterous existence it had been before. War had wrought subtle changes just as it had with other American families. In Hyannis Port or Bronxville—

wherever the Kennedys were staying—an atmosphere of restlessness and uncertainty about the future now hung over the household.

Jack's request for combat duty finally came through. In early March of 1943, he was sent to San Diego where he boarded a Navy transport and watched pensively from the deck as a golden sun bathed the disappearing California coast in an unreal glow.

At Espíritu Santo, a beautiful tropical island a thousand miles north of Australia, he was transferred to a Navy landing ship, LST 449, which was to take him to his destination, the PT-boat base at Tulagi, an island just north of Guadalcanal in the Solomon Islands chain.

The Solomons were the pivotal point of the Pacific War at this time. Tulagi, prewar capital of the British Solomon Islands, had been seized by the Japanese five months after Pearl Harbor, but in August, 1942, the Americans relanded on Guadalcanal. After bloody fighting, the Japanese were forced to withdraw from "The Canal" and from neighboring Tulagi, a narrow, hilly island which was soon converted into PT-boat headquarters. Here there were repair shops, mooring berths, a supply depot and living quarters for the officers and crews.

The entire Allied offensive in the Pacific was now being concentrated against New Georgia, Rendova and other islands in the Solomon chain northwest of Guadalcanal and Tulagi. According to the American strategy, driving the Japanese out of the Solomons was to be the first step in an Allied effort to regain control of the South Pacific and obtain a springboard for the invasion of Japan itself.

In the early afternoon of April 7, 1943, LST 449

approached the northern coast of Guadalcanal. Jack was below, propped up in his bunk reading. Suddenly he noticed that the vessel had begun to roll sharply, as if circling. Springing out of bed he started for the deck, and just as he got to the head of the gangway, he was thrown off his feet by a violent explosion. At the same time an acrid odor of gunpowder assailed his nostrils, and he knew instinctively that the ship was being attacked.

Scrambling out on deck, he saw a fantastic sight. Japanese planes were hurtling in from every direction, and a nearby American destroyer, which he assumed had been sent out to escort LST 449 into Guadalcanal, was also under attack.

Taking cover in a gangway, he saw red flame and great black billows of smoke rising from the escort destroyer which had sustained a direct hit. It was obvious the destroyer did not stand a chance, and later he learned that she had gone down three miles from shore.

Soon the enemy planes veered off, climbed for the sky and disappeared—the air attack was over. Someone on deck shouted that two Japanese pilots had parachuted into the water and that one of them was just east of the ship. LST 449 headed toward the flier. Jack joined dozens of other soldiers and sailors at the rail to watch the rescue.

As a precaution, in case the Japanese pilot attempted to resist, the 449's executive officer armed himself with a submachine gun and stood on the starboard side of the bridge, his weapon at the ready. The enemy flier floated in his life jacket passively enough until the LST was within a few yards. Then he began to swim away.

Someone threw a rope into the sea. At that moment

the downed pilot turned, jerked a revolver from beneath the water and fired twice at the rescue party on 449. Both shots missed, and before he could press the trigger again, there was a rapid burst of fire from the submachine gun. As the shots struck the Japanese, he raised both arms as if to ward off the bullets and fell face forward in the water. In stunned disbelief Jack stared at the floating body of the dead man, then turned away with a helpless, sinking feeling in the pit of his stomach.

Shortly after reporting to the commanding officer of the Tulagi PT-boat base, Jack was assigned as skipper of a boat whose crew had just completed a tour of combat duty and was scheduled to return to the United States. The boat was known as PT 109.

The craft turned out to be a far cry from the clean, new boats at Mellville. She had been in combat for nine months and had scars to prove it. Encrusted with dirt and grime, she had become a haven for cockroaches and rats. Nevertheless, Jack swallowed his disappointment and concentrated on the all-important task of picking a crew which normally consisted of an executive officer and ten enlisted men, in addition to the skipper. Because of a shortage of replacements, he was told he would have to do with only nine enlisted men.

In his choice of an "exec," luck was with him, for he inherited Ensign Leonard Thom, a huge former football star from Ohio State University who had served under PT 109's former skipper, Lieutenant (jg) Bryant L. Larson, but had not completed his combat tour. The rest of the boat's complement had to be taken from a replacement roster of unknowns as combat-green as himself. In making his choice, Jack tried to select men who seemed genial and dependable, for a

PT crew, like a bomber's, had to operate as a tightly coordinated team.

The crew he finally picked ranged in age from nineteen to thirty-two and consisted of Ensign Thom, Gunner's Mates Charles A. Harris and Maurice L. Kowal; Motor Machinist's Mates Leon E. Drawdy, Edmund T. Drewitch, William Johnson and Patrick Henry McMahon; Torpedoman Andrew Jackson Kirksey; Radioman John E. Maguire; and Seaman Edgar E. Mauer, who was to serve as a jack-of-all-trades—quartermaster, signalman, cook and odd-job man.

For the first few weeks there were nightly patrols in the vicinity of tiny Savo Island, a spit of land guarding the water approach to Guadalcanal and Tulagi. Fortunately, these were without incident, for the war by now had moved two hundred miles northwest—to Rendova, New Georgia and the other islands of the western Solomons.

The days at Tulagi were spent trying to make life more livable. The heat was overpowering, the tiny huts that served as living quarters were primitive, and the food monotonous. Mostly they ate Spam—a canned meat hash that tasted the same day in and day out in spite of Ed Mauer's best culinary efforts to disguise it. Occasionally, Jack picked up advance word of the arrival of a Navy cargo ship, and he raced out on 109 with throttles wide open to meet the incoming vessel. Such initiative usually paid off in candy bars, soap, fresh bread or, if luck truly smiled on them, a dozen eggs.

Jack was well liked among the base personnel. Some of the officers, like George "Barney" Ross, had gone through training with him, so it was no secret that he was the son of the famous Joseph P. Kennedy. Nevertheless, his lack of affectation made him popular with his fellow officers and the enlisted men. Tulagi was no place for Navy spit and polish, so Jack wore the unofficial uniform of the base, stripped to the waist with a sheath knife in his belt, sunglasses and a long-visored fatigue or baseball cap.

Although he frequently played cards with his fellow officers and enjoyed discussing politics with them, most of his time was spent with his own men. The relationship between crew members on a PT-boat was a close one, like that on a bomber. In the tightly compressed quarters aboard ship and the split-second teamwork necessary for survival, distinctions of rank often broke down, and competence and fairness were considered the important attributes for engendering respect. Measured by this yardstick, Jack was rated highly by his own crew who boasted to their fellow enlisted men that he was the best skipper on Tulagi.

In mid-July of 1943, Jack and some of the other skippers received orders to proceed to Rendova in the western Solomon Islands for combat duty! Two weeks earlier, American troops had succeeded in driving the Japanese off Rendova which was now being set up as a base for air and sea operations against the enemy.

The two-hundred-mile run to the western Solomons took the 109 ten hours. Rendova Harbor was a two-mile stretch of placid blue water. At its northern end was a 1,500-foot kidney-shaped strip of land known as Lumberi Island which served as the PT-boat mooring area.

From Lieutenant Commander Thomas G. Warfield, commanding officer of the PT flotilla, Jack and the others learned what their mission was to be. Rendova was just south of two islands named Kolombangara and Vella Lavella, both Japanese held. Kolombangara was of particular importance, for it supplied enemy holdouts on New Georgia Island where bloody fighting was still taking place.

Supplies were shipped to Kolombangara and Vella Lavella by night convoy from the great Japanese base at Rabaul, on New Britain Island to the north. These ships, usually destroyers, had been dubbed "The Tokyo Express" by the Americans. They made their way south through Japanese-controlled waters, then waited for the cover of darkness to sneak into a stretch of sea known as Blackett Strait which separated Kolombangara and Vella Lavella. Once they negotiated the strait, they were free to discharge their supplies and make the run back to Rabaul.

The task of the Rendova PT-boat squadron was to intercept the cargo-laden ships of "The Tokyo Express" in Blackett Strait and starve the Japanese bases on Kolombangara and Vella Lavella into surrender, thereby leading to American control of the entire Solomon chain! The patrol route would take the PT-boats from Rendova northwest into open water through the Solomon Sea, at which point they would swing northeast through Ferguson Passage, a broad channel running between the sea and Blackett Strait. Once in the strait, the boats would patrol all night in search of enemy shipping.

Jack discovered that plying the waters of Blackett Strait at night was a far cry from the peaceful patrols off Tulagi where the absence of the enemy was almost taken for granted. At Blackett Strait brushes with Japanese destroyers and aircraft were so common that scarcely a night went by without at least one PT-boat sustaining damage from enemy shells or bombs.

On July 19, after a week of patrols in which PT 109 had not suffered even a scratch, a Japanese fighter plane spotted the boat in semidarkness and dropped two bombs a short distance off the port beam. Flying shrapnel blew a hole in the 109's hull and wounded Motor Machinist's Mate Drawdy in the left arm and Gunner's Mate Kowal in the ankle. Although the wounds were not serious, the doctors at Rendova decided to hospitalize the men. Accordingly, Jack replaced them with two newcomers to Rendova—Gerard E. Zinser, a career Navy man from California, and Harold Marney, a youngster of nineteen from Massachusetts. In addition, Lieutenant Commander Warfield agreed to assign a tenth enlisted man to complete the boat's complement—Torpedoman Raymond Starkey, a cynical but experienced combat veteran, who had asked to be transferred from another crew because of a personality clash with his skipper. Jack soon found that by giving him responsibility and displaying a sense of humor in his dealings with him, Starkey could be relied on to do his job efficiently.

As July drew to an end, the Japanese stepped up their desperate effort to retain a foothold on New Georgia Island and thus block American attempts to take over the entire Solomon chain. On August 1, Warfield received word that a large Japanese convoy was expected to run Blackett Strait that night. He was ordered to put all available PT-boats into action.

That afternoon a large squadron of Japanese planes bombed and strafed Rendova in an obvious attempt to knock the flotilla out of commission. Fortunately, the damage was minor and fifteen boats remained available for the night's mission, but it did serve to confirm the earlier intelligence report that the enemy was up to something big.

At the briefing that afternoon, Commander Warfield laid out the plan for the night's patrol. All fifteen boats would be used, thus making it one of the major PT actions of the war. They would be divided into divisions, with each division responsible for a given area.

PT 109 was to be the last boat in Division "B," led by Lieutenant Henry J. Brantingham, skipper of PT 159. The others in "B" were PT 157 and PT 162. The division would patrol the point farthest north in Blackett Strait, thereby placing it in the likeliest position to encounter the enemy convoy heading south.

On his way to the 109 Jack met Barney Ross. Ross had no assignment because his boat had been sunk accidentally by American bombers ten days before. Smelling excitement, he pleaded with Jack to let him go along on the 109 that night.

Jack was pleased to have an extra hand on board. "Can you fire a 37-millimeter gun, Barney?" he asked.

"Not exactly, but I can learn," Ross replied confidently.

"Okay, you're signed on then."

Just before dusk, Rendova Harbor came to life with the roar of PT engines. Jack could sense that his crew was more nervous than at any time in the recent past. The promise of a dangerous mission, preceded by the air raid in the afternoon, had made everyone edgy.

He himself felt tense and uncertain about this mission. A crew member, Torpedoman Andy Kirksey, had let it be known that he had a premonition of death. Since Kirksey was normally one of the steadiest men on board, this unnerved the rest of the crew. Jack and some of the others tried to reassure Kirksey but it did no good. When he was offered the chance to skip the patrol, Kirksey refused, protesting that he didn't want anyone to think he was "yellow."

The boats were mustering into division now. Jack was last in line in Division "B"—behind 159, 157 and 162. Slowly, the tiny flotilla headed out into open water.

By 9:30 P.M. they had cleared Ferguson Passage and were heading straight toward their assigned patrol area in Blackett Strait. According to plan, Lieutenant Brantingham's 159 had paired off with 157, while 109 was paired with 162. Jack tried to keep as close as possible to his partner, but it was so dark that he could barely make out PT 162. It was on such nights that he wished 109 had a radar set on board, like Brantingham's boat and some of the others. Without radar it was impossible to detect other craft even a short distance away.

The procedure was for PT 162 to keep tuned to Brantingham's boat by radio and pass any instructions along to 109. However, as the patrol continued, there were no messages at all on the radio. They had lost contact.

By now neither Jack nor Lieutenant John Lowrey, skipper of 162, had the faintest notion of where Brantingham's boat and its partner PT 157 had gone. Jack was suddenly aware of flashes of light in the general direction of Kolombangara Island. He suspected they were shore batteries firing on the PT boats, but it was only a guess. One time, a searchlight beam came close to 109, and a couple of shells fell nearby. He ordered "general quarters" and the crew sprang to battle stations. Lowrey, the section leader, realizing that he had come dangerously within range of enemy guns, swung away and churned north up Blackett Strait with Jack following closely in his wake. A little later Jack pulled alongside 162 and asked Lowrey if he had any idea what was happening. The other skipper shook his head.

Jack's radioman, Johnny Maguire, tuned in the 109's radio on the general frequency and reported he could hear all sorts of strange messages like, "Am being chased." "Have fired fish." "Get out of there as fast as you can." Jack checked again with Lowrey who had heard the same thing. It was very confusing, but the two youthful skippers could only guess that some of the boats were engaged in an action somewhere.

PT 162 and PT 109 continued up Blackett Strait. All of a sudden, they encountered PT 169 from Division "A" which had also lost contact with its leader. Lieutenant Potter, the 169's skipper, was as confused as Jack and Lowrey, and since the original plan had obviously broken down, the three agreed to wait it out together until they received orders by radio.

Cutting their motors down to idling, Jack, Lowrey and Potter listened impatiently for instructions. None came. Finally Lowrey agreed to call Rendova for orders. Rendova headquarters, thirty-eight miles away, directed them to continue their patrol. By this time, no one remembered from which direction they had come. They had changed course so many times that it was impossible to estimate position by dead reckoning, and since it was pitch black there was no way of obtaining a "fix" from coastal landmarks.

For the next several hours, the three boats patrolled back and forth on a blind course. Each skipper took his turn leading the others. By now it was two-thirty in the morning. PT 109 was in the lead of a straggling formation, with Barney Ross on the bow as lookout. Suddenly, a ghostly shape emerged from the darkness no more than two or three hundred yards off 109's starboard bow. At first glance, it seemed to be another PT boat, coming directly at them at top speed. Ross shouted, "Ship at two o'clock!"

Jack stared at the oncoming craft and recognized it as a Japanese destroyer! He swung hard on the right rudder, to position himself for a torpedo attack. Unfortunately, 109 had been running on one engine and responded sluggishly to the wheel.

The prow of the Japanese ship sliced into the fragile PT boat like a warm knife into a stick of butter.

The wheel was torn from Jack's grasp and he was hurled against the rear of the cockpit, his back slamming against a steel brace. Then he felt his legs give way and he found himself lying on the deck. Looking up, he stared in horrified disbelief as the huge bow of the destroyer swept past, ripping his boat in two with a sickening, splintering noise.

High-octane fuel had escaped and the water near the boat was on fire. The 109 was illuminated by the light of a river of flames only a few yards away.

Jack dragged himself to his feet and stared weakly at an incredible sight. The afterpart of the boat had been completely sheared away, and only the forward half on which most of the crew had been stationed was still afloat. In addition to himself, three men were still on board. The rest must have been hurled into the water, he told himself groggily.

Fearing that the flames on the water might spread to the floating bow and cause a gasoline tank to explode or that the enemy might fire on them if members of the crew were seen on the bow, Jack ordered everyone into the water.

He and the others swam a short distance away and waited, floating in their kapok life vests. The flames soon died out, and the enemy ship seemed to have disappeared into the night's blackness. Jack led the others back to the floating bow and they climbed aboard.

He shouted for survivors and there were several weak answering voices. Ed Mauer got out a blinker light. Guided by the beam, Jack dropped off the floating hull and swam toward the voices. He found two enlisted men, Charley Harris, a fellow Bostonian, and Pat McMahon. The latter was badly burned. Jack instructed him to float on his back and towed him to the hull. Then he returned for Harris who was complaining that he had injured his leg and couldn't swim.

"Try," Jack urged.

"I can't."

"For a guy from Boston, you're certainly putting up a great exhibition out here," Jack retorted in weary disgust.

He grabbed Harris and towed him toward the 109 which was drifting farther and farther away. It was slow, torturously wearying work. After what seemed like years, he managed to fight his way to the hull with Harris in tow.

Meanwhile, other survivors, guided by Mauer's signal, had managed to swim to the 109. They helped each other aboard. Jack took count. Besides himself, ten men were on the floating bow. Two enlisted men were missing—Kirksey, who had had the premonition of death, and Harold Marney, the new man who had been Kowal's replacement.

For half an hour they shouted, but there was no answer. They knew then that both men had perished.

Someone thought to ask where the two other PT boats had gone, for they had disappeared at the time of the collision. One of the crew members cursed the other skippers for not waiting around to rescue them, but Jack explained that in all probability they had seen the flames and were convinced that an explosion had taken the lives of all on board. The PT 109 survivors discussed their plight and assured each other that when morning came they would be spotted and rescued.

As the pink glow of dawn painted the horizon, they waited impatiently for help to arrive. They waited and waited. None came.

7

PACIFIC ORDEAL

Jack examined their predicament realistically. In almost every direction, there were islands crawling with Japanese. What if they had to fight? He took inventory and found that they had one submachine gun, six .45-caliber automatics, his own .38 revolver and two standard issue jungle knives. With such weapons they could hardly put up a spirited defense.

Furthermore, the hulk was beginning to settle in the water, and it was obvious they could not stay on it much longer. He decided that since there was no means of propelling it to shore, their best bet was to swim to safety. But where?

Having covered the area almost nightly on patrol missions, he had used many of the islands as navigational landmarks. He recognized the closest as Kolombangara, only two and a half miles to the east, but that was Japanese held. Some three and a half miles to the west, though, was a group of small islands that overlooked Ferguson Passage. And the PT squadrons went through the passage every night! One of these might offer an excellent vantage point from which to signal a passing boat.

Jack chose Plum Pudding Island, a tiny knuckle of land large enough to conceal eleven men, but too small to serve as a base for enemy soldiers, and pointed it out to the men. "How do we get there?" someone asked.

"We swim," Jack said.

But it was not that simple. Some of the men were better swimmers than others. In addition, McMahon, who was horribly burnt, was completely helpless. While pondering the problem of how to keep the crew together, Jack's eyes fell on a two-by-eight-inch plank in the water. It was tied to the bow. The board had been used as a makeshift base for a 37-millimeter deck gun. During the collision it had been hurled into the sea where it had floated all night. Why couldn't the plank be used as a mammoth life preserver?

Under his direction, the men removed their shoes and tied them to the plank. They also tied their weapons, a rubber life belt, the ship's lantern and a powerful ten-pound flashlight wrapped in kapok to the floating timber.

Everybody except him and McMahon would swim together by hanging onto the plank and kicking, Jack explained. The men on the ends would also use one free arm to paddle. In that way, the strong swimmers would be helping the weak, and the crew would stay together. Ensign Thom would be in charge.

Since McMahon was incapable even of hanging onto the plank because of his burns, he would have to be towed all the way. "I'll take McMahon with me," Jack said matter-of-factly.

After seeing the rest of his men off, he gently helped McMahon into the water and slid off the hulk himself. On the back of the burned man's kapok life vest was a three-foot strap which could be used as a towrope. Jack grasped the strap in his teeth and started swimming, using an easy breast stroke, with McMahon floating behind in helpless silence.

For the next four hours the small caravan of survivors made its way across Blackett Strait toward Plum Pudding Island. In the beginning Jack and the men on the plank managed to stay together; but eventually he began to pull ahead, in spite of having McMahon in tow. His progress was in spurts—he swam for ten or fifteen minutes, paused to rest, then swam again.

As the afternoon wore on, the sun grew hotter, and the glaring rays were blinding. He was conscious of a painful sensation in his back, where he had struck the steel cockpit brace during the collision, and he wondered if he had aggravated his old football injury. Moreover, because of the belt between his teeth he found himself swallowing massive quantities of sea water, and he was beginning to feel ill.

Now he could make out the green branches of the trees on Plum Pudding Island. He forgot his pain temporarily in his eagerness to reach the objective. His arms were so paralyzed with weariness that they seemed no longer to belong to him, yet he kept up a steady stroke, keeping his attention fixed on a particular bush near a white sandy strip of beach to mark his progress.

When at last he could feel his feet touching bottom, he painfully dragged himself and McMahon forward by sheer dint of will until they were on the beach. Then he released the strap and collapsed just beyond the point where the surf bubbled up on the clean white beach.

He lay there panting, his head buried in the moist sand. McMahon, who was crawling on his knees, tried to help him up, but his burnt hands were swollen to grotesque size and he was helpless. Finally Jack staggered to his feet and began to vomit from the sea water he had swallowed during the four-hour ordeal.

After a short pause to regain his strength, he crawled with McMahon across the beach to a covering of small bushes. McMahon lay stretched out on the ground. Breathing heavily, his back throbbing with pain, Jack sat and watched the progress of the nine men on the plank as they neared the island.

When finally they gained the beach, he waved feebly and signaled them to take cover. They ducked behind a clump of trees and circled around to where he and McMahon were waiting.

Suddenly there was the sound of a motor in the distance. Although the bushes offered excellent cover, everyone practically stopped breathing. Jack peered cautiously through the vegetation. Not more than two hundred yards away, a motorized barge labored through the surf, manned by Japanese! The Americans waited fearfully, not daring to move a muscle. The enemy craft passed by slowly and finally disappeared.

Jack called a council of war, and the crew members discussed their plight in hushed tones. There was no food or fresh water and only a few weapons. But on the positive side, they were on a tiny island only a hundred yards long and seventy yards wide at its broadest point. While too small for the enemy to bother about, the island had trees and bushes for concealment. Most heartening of all, it was located reasonably close to the juncture of Blackett Strait and Ferguson Passage, not far from the nightly regular PT route.

Jack called Ensigns Ross and Thom aside for a high-level strategy meeting and laid an idea before them.

Why couldn't he swim out into the passage that night with the 109's lantern and try to intercept one of the PT-boats from Rendova? Yes, he knew it would be hard for a swimmer to stop a PT-boat in the dark unless it was very close by, but he could take his pistol along to attract the crew's attention and flash the lantern.

Ross's comment was brief and blunt. "It's crazy. It'll never work, Jack." Thom merely shook his head, as if convinced that his skipper had lost his wits.

In spite of their lack of enthusiasm, Jack informed the rest of the crew of his plan. Pat McMahon feebly retorted that Mr. Kennedy seemed eager to commit suicide.

Undeterred, Jack stripped down to his shorts, tied the rubber life belt around his middle and hung his 38 around his neck with a lanyard. Then he wrapped the lantern in kapok so it would float and tied it to his life belt. The sun was just fading below the horizon when he walked into the surf and made his way to a coral reef which rimmed the island. His maps, he recalled, had indicated that the reef extended southward for a considerable distance, eventually forming the northern boundary of Ferguson Passage. His plan was to proceed along the reef as far as possible, until it touched the passage, then swim out into the middle of the passage and float until the PT's came up from Rendova on their nightly run.

The depth of water along the reef varied. Sometimes it was waist deep, at other times it covered his shoulders. Occasionally, it was too deep for him to walk, so he had to swim. As darkness came, the silence was intense and he felt lost in an endless desert of eerie loneliness.

After two or three miles, he reached the passage. Floating himself off the reef he struck out for the middle of the channel. The water was generally warm, although occasionally there were cold patches that left him breathless. He strained to hear the sound of motors, but heard only the gentle lapping of the waves.

Upon reaching the middle of the passage he began to tread water, waiting hopefully. No PT-boats came. To the north, beyond an island called Gizo, he saw aerial flares, and a terrifying suspicion began to haunt him. Quite often the boats from Lumberi were assigned to patrol Gizo Strait instead of Blackett Strait. Could that have been the case tonight? If so, his long trek and swim from Plum Pudding Island would have been in vain.

Yet in spite of his growing sense of futility he could not be certain, so he continued to maintain his wet, lonely vigil in the middle of Ferguson Passage. He floated or treaded water most of the time, occasionally paddling around to keep his arms and legs from cramping up. The .38 hanging from the lanyard around his neck felt like a ton of dead weight. But there was neither sound nor sign of a boat.

Finally, after what seemed an eternity, he knew that it was hopeless. The PT's, for some reason or other, were not moving through Ferguson Passage this night. Conscious of the acute pain in his back and bone weary, he began to paddle in what he thought was the direction of the coral reef. He swam on and on, gingerly testing the water's depth every few minutes to see if he had gained the reef. As the hours passed, and he still could not touch the coral with his feet, he knew that he was lost. However, there was nothing to do but go on.

As early morning came, a pale dawn illumined the vast watery world in which he had been swimming all night. He found to his dismay that he was still in the middle of Ferguson Passage, but much farther east. Apparently, a current had carried him up to Blackett Strait, and this explained why he had never reached the reef.

Off in the distance, in the direction of the reef, he saw a tiny island which he recalled from his Navy maps as Leorava. Actually, it was a minute speck of land with a single tree and a patch of bushes, but it was a place to go and rest. So with his last remaining strength, he paddled toward it and finally pulled himself up on shore. Then he collapsed on his stomach and went to sleep.

When he awoke the sun was high overhead, set against a deep blue sky. He felt cold and ill. And ahead of him was a mile and a half swim to Plum Pudding Island.

Once he was in the water, he felt warmer, but the nausea was still with him, and it grew worse with each mouthful of salt water that he swallowed. He reached Plum Pudding in late morning. Ross and Thom rushed out on the beach to greet him. Ross threw his arms around him and asked if he had seen any PT boats. Jack shook his head in reply and fell to his knees, sick to his stomach. Afterward, he fell asleep without a word.

He awoke briefly in the afternoon and suggested that Ross, who was the best swimmer of the crew next to himself, try Ferguson Passage that night. Ross was convinced that it was useless, but he dutifully obeyed. Taking Jack's .38 and a life belt, he waded into the surf and soon disappeared in the distance.

The next morning Jack opened his eyes feeling a lot better. The pain in his back had subsided a bit. A little later Ross returned and reported that his vigil had been as unsuccessful as Jack's. Curiously, it turned out that he, too, had stumbled across Leorava Island and had spent the night there.

Jack was hungry and thirsty, for he had not had anything to eat or drink since before the collision. His stomach felt pinched and his throat was parched. He learned that in his absence the men had found a few coconuts and had eaten the meat and drunk the milk. Seaman Ed Mauer, who had served as the 109's cook, hacked a coconut open and gave it to Jack. He found it surprisingly good.

Afterward they held another strategy meeting. Jack decided that it would be better to move to Olasana, an island a mile and a half away. Olasana was closer to Ferguson Passage, and he explained that it would improve their chances of being spotted. Furthermore, it was larger than Plum Pudding Island and thus a better source of coconuts, for Mauer was complaining that the available supply on Plum Island was just about exhausted.

They dragged their plank into the water and used the same procedure they had followed in swimming from the hulk of PT 109. Jack again towed McMahon by his kapok strap. Because of strong currents it took several hours to make the crossing, but once they neared Olasana their spirits rose, for it abounded in coconut palms.

Jack and McMahon reached the beach first. When the men on the plank finally made shore a brief meeting was held. They were so weary that Jack decided not to send anyone into Ferguson Passage that night. Instead they huddled together for warmth and went to sleep immediately.

The next morning was August 5. Four nights had passed since PT 109 had gone down, yet it seemed as if they had been castaways forever. They looked across a half-mile stretch of water to a neighboring island, Naru. On the far side of this little island was Ferguson Passage itself. Jack suggested that he and Ross swim to Naru for a "quick look around."

After the long swims of the previous days the half-mile crossing required relatively little exertion. Upon reaching the shore the two made for the nearest cluster of trees and headed for the far side of the island. They moved stealthily for there was always the chance that Naru was being used by the Japanese as an observation base.

After satisfying themselves that the place was deserted, they began a systematic exploration. Off in the distance across Ferguson Passage was towering Rendova Peak, on their home island. They could not help wondering what the PT crews were doing at that precise moment, and whether they would ever get to see them again. The peak was thirty-eight miles away, yet it seemed close enough to reach out and touch.

A little way down the beach they made a fascinating discovery. On the coral reef, not more than a mile from shore, was the wreckage of a small Japanese boat. It looked as though it had been thoroughly clobbered in a strafing attack. Excited by their find, they quickened their pace and a few hundred yards farther on they struck gold. Some cargo had apparently been washed ashore from the Japanese craft! They eagerly broke open a crate and found a store of hard sugar candy. Stuffing their mouths with sweets, they continued their exploration, after agreeing that they would return later to devise a method for floating the crate of candy back to Olasana.

They walked another twenty yards and caught sight of an object through a clump of bushes. It was a native dugout canoe containing a large tin of rain water. They glanced at each other triumphantly. Jack swooped down on the container, took a swig, then passed it to Ross who drank deeply.

Just as Ross put down the tin, they noticed movement on the Japanese wreck on the reef. Paralyzed with fear, they stared across the mile of water at a chilling sight. Two men were standing on the deck of the hulk and seemed to be peering at them!

Jack and Ross dived into the bushes and lay deathly still, observing the wreckage. Had they been spotted? It was obvious that they had, for the two men, whose features they could not make out in the distance, leaped into a small boat and paddled away furiously.

After remaining hidden for some minutes to make sure the strangers did not return, Jack and Ross agreed that they were probably natives and decided to continue their exploration. The discovery of the canoe had given an entirely different perspective to their problem. With a boat they were mobile; they could go for help, or they could maintain a nightly vigil in Ferguson Passage until PT boats arrived. Thus for the first time in days, Jack felt in high spirits.

He decided that their first task was to bring the candy and water to the men on Olasana. Tearing a slat off one of the cargo crates for a paddle, he told Ross to wait on Naru until he returned. "I'll be back as soon as I can," he promised. "It'll be dusk by then and we can go out to the middle of the passage."

Traveling by canoe, Jack decided, was far easier than swimming. He grinned as he anticipated his triumphant arrival in the tiny craft and the amazed looks on the faces of the men. But when he reached the beach it was *he* who was amazed. The crew rushed out excitedly to greet him, but they hardly noticed the boat. Instead they introduced him to two natives who had been paddling by Olasana Island in a canoe and had stopped to find fresh water to drink. While the natives did not speak English, Jack realized later that they were the same two men he and Ross had spied on board the Japanese hulk!

In spite of this new development, Jack decided that their best bet still was the possibility of intercepting a PT boat in Ferguson Passage. Accordingly he told the men that he would return the following morning, and paddled off in his canoe to Naru Island.

Ross was not at all enthusiastic about venturing out in the passage, for the water seemed rough that evening, but Jack pointed out that the sturdy native canoes were built to withstand storms. Still dubious, Ross finally agreed to go. A few hundred years from shore giant waves began to wash over the gunwales and the canoe bobbed about like a cork.

Before Jack could decide whether to turn back, a huge wave spun the craft around. They were hurled into the water and the canoe capsized. The next thing he knew, he and Ross were hanging onto the overturned boat for dear life.

It was getting dark, but by hard swimming they managed to work the canoe in the general direction of Naru Island. The vigorous activity caused Jack's back to throb again. The pounding waves swept them and the overturned boat across the reef and into the protected shallows. Thoroughly exhausted, they crawled up on the beach and went to sleep.

The next morning they returned to Olasana. For an hour or so, everybody sat around and discussed plans. Now that they had two canoes—their own and that of the natives—how could they best use them? It was finally agreed that the natives should be sent to Rendova to bring back help. Jack used sign language to persuade one of them to paddle across to Naru with him. There in the distance, thirty-eight miles away, was majestic Rendova Peak. By vigorous signs, he managed to convey the idea that he wished the native to paddle there by canoe. The islander, who had given the Americans to understand that his name was Biuku, nodded. Jack picked up a coconut and motioned to Biuku to split it. The native did so expertly, using a sharpened peg. On a piece of the shell, Jack scratched the following message with his sheath knife:

NARU ISL

NATIVE KNOWS POSIT
HE CAN PILOT   11 ALIVE NEED
SMALL BOAT

They returned to Olasana Island where Jack found that Ensign Thom had also been at work preparing a message. Thom had found a pencil stub in one of his pockets as well as an old invoice blank which he had picked up somewhere. His message read:

To: Commanding Officer—Oak o
From: Crew P.T. 109 (Oak 14)
Subject: Rescue of 11 (eleven) men lost since Sunday, Aug 1st in enemy action. Native knows

our position & will bring PT boat back to small islands of Ferguson Passage off NARU IS.

A small boat (outboard or oars) is needed to take men off as some are seriously burned

Signal at night—three dashes(- - -)

Password—Roger—Answer—Wilco

If attempted at day time—advise air coverage or a PBY could set down. Please work out suitable plan & act immediately. Help is urgent & in sore need.

Rely on native boys to any extent

> *L. J. Thom*
> *Ens. U.S.N.R.*
> *Exec. 109*

They decided to send both messages. Jack's coconut shell and Thom's invoice were entrusted to Biuku and the other islander whose name was Eroni. The natives jumped into their canoe and paddled off with amazing speed. Jack and the others sat down on the beach and watched the craft disappear in the distance, wondering if they would ever hear from Biuku and Eroni again.

Early the next morning Jack was awakened by the rustling of a nearby bush. He stealthily reached for his .38. The others had also heard the noise and were waiting silently, expectantly, gripping their pistols and knives.

Suddenly the bushes parted and a husky native entered the clearing, followed by half a dozen others. He was naked except for a cloth around his waist. Bowing slightly, he said with a clipped British accent, "I have a letter for the senior officer."

Astounded, Jack got up and identified himself. He thanked the native and tore the message open. It read:

ON HIS MAJESTY'S SERVICE

To senior officer, Naru Is.

Friday 11 P.M. Have just learnt of your presence on Naru Is. & also that two natives have taken news to Rendova. I strongly advise you return immediately to here in this canoe & by the time you arrive here I will be in Radio communication with authorities at Rendova & we can finalise plans to collect balance your party.

A. R. Evans Lt.
R A N V R

Will warn aviation of your crossing Ferguson Passage

From Benjamin Kevu, the half-naked islander who spoke superb English, Jack obtained the rest of the story. Lieutenant Evans, a coastwatcher or observer for the Australian Navy, operated from Gomu Island under the eyes of the enemy with native help. Kevu and the others were Evans' scouts. Biuku and Eroni, who knew Benjamin Kevu, had stopped off briefly to tell him about the PT 109 party before going on to Rendova. Kevu, in turn, had informed Evans who had dispatched him and the others to locate the survivors.

The large native outrigger canoe in which Kevu and the other scouts had come was loaded with food. The eleven famished Americans ate with such gluttony that their rescuers could only stare in disbelief. There were potatoes, yams, pawpaws, rice, boiled fish, tinned roast beef hash and even cigarettes.

During the meal Jack discussed the situation with Thom and Ross. It was agreed that he would follow Evans' suggestion to go with the natives to meet Evans and work out a rescue plan. The Australian was at Gomu Island, about two hours away. During the trip Jack stayed well down, hidden by palm fronds. Several Japanese planes passed close by but ignored the native outrigger.

When they approached Gomu Beach, Lieutenant Evans was waiting to greet them. Jack stuck his head up through the palm fronds. "Hello," he grinned. "I'm Kennedy." Evans, a wiry, light-complexioned Australian in his thirties, replied, "Come and have some tea."

The plan they worked out was simple enough. Evans would radio a message to Lumberi asking that a PT boat be dispatched to rendezvous with Jack later that evening. The rendezvous point would be nearby Patparan Island, rather than Gomu, in order to protect Lieutenant Evans. Jack and he knew that if the Japanese spotted activity at Gomu and investigated they would surely discover the coast-watching station. Evans sent the message immediately, noting that the recognition signal would be four revolver shots.

A little after eight o'clock the scouts paddled Jack to Patparan. They waited in the dark. Suddenly, at about ten o'clock, Jack heard the familiar rumble of PT engines. Then there were four shots. He replied by firing in the air four times. A dark shape emerged from the night, and the natives paddled forward until they were along the starboard side of the PT. "Hey, Jack," someone called. He recognized the voice immediately as that of Lieutenant Bill Liebenow, skipper of PT 157.

"Where in blazes have you been?" Jack inquired in mock anger.

"Want something to eat?" one of the men aboard the PT offered.

"No, thanks," Jack retorted wryly. "I just had a

coconut." A short time later PT 157, directed by Jack, made its way to Olasana. Biuku and Eroni were on board and helped bring the rest of the 109 survivors off the island. Then Lieutenant Liebenow headed back for Lumberi. They chugged into Rendova Harbor just as dawn was breaking. The date was Sunday, August 8, 1943.

Their seven-day ordeal was over.

The crew was shipped to the Navy hospital at Tulagi. The doctors assured them that all would recover, including badly burned McMahon. Since they had been reported missing, word was now sent to their families that they had been found. The Navy doctors discovered that Jack had ruptured his disc during the ramming of PT 109. He was informed that he was being recommended for the Purple Heart because the injury had been sustained in action. And he and Thom were also awarded the Navy and Marine Corps Medal for gallantry in saving their men. Furthermore, Jack received a promotion to the rank of full lieutenant.

According to Navy custom, men who had been shipwrecked were permitted to go home. However, Jack told his superiors that he did not want to go back and asked to be assigned to another boat.

Upon returning to his base from the sick bay at Tulagi he was given PT 59 which had been converted into a gunboat for action against enemy barges. Five of his old crew volunteered to serve with him in his new command.

For the next three months, Jack and the others saw action almost daily as the struggle for control of the Solomon Islands intensified. On November 2, he nosed PT 59 into a coral reef at Choiseul, one of the islands still under control of the Japanese, to evacuate an invasion force of fifty marines who had been cut off by enemy reinforcements. The rescue was successful, although one badly wounded marine died on board.

Jack received numerous letters from home giving him all the family gossip. His younger brother, Robert, seventeen, had enlisted in the Navy; and Kick was definitely planning to marry young William Cavendish, the Marquess of Hartington, who was now a captain in Britain's famous Coldstream Guards.

In his letters, Jack tried to sound light and cheerful, for he sensed that his folks had not yet fully recovered from the shock of being told that he was missing in action. But in truth, things were not going as well as he tried to pretend. The injury to his back and the strain of his many hours in the water had resulted in complications. His back pained him much of the time now, and he was told that the swimming had damaged his adrenal glands. Additional examination by the Navy doctors disclosed that he had ruptured the disc between his fifth vertebra and sacrum, at the lower spine, thus aggravating his earlier football injury. Moreover, he had contracted malaria, probably as a result of not having taken Atabrine during the week of his ordeal.

Early in November, the doctors announced that he was no longer in physical condition to continue on combat status. On November 18, 1943, he bade a sad farewell to his crew and boarded a transport plane to fly back to the States.

He was assigned as an instructor in a PT training program in Miami, Florida. It was a pleasant enough life, particularly since it was only a short distance from the family's Palm Beach home. The reunion with his parents was a warm one. The Ambassador and Mrs. Kennedy said little, but from the way his father shook his hand and his mother kissed and hugged him Jack knew that they had never expected to see him again.

The duty at Miami lasted for almost six months. Jack had hoped that his back would improve sufficiently to enable him to apply for overseas duty, but he was doomed to disappointment. The pain grew steadily worse. And his malaria was acting up so badly that his weight dropped to a mere one hundred and twenty-five pounds. Late in the spring, he entered the Chelsea Naval Hospital near Boston to find out if his back could be cured or if he was doomed to be an invalid for the rest of his life.

8

ON THE HUSTINGS

The Navy doctors were in disagreement as to a course of action. Jack's back had sustained serious injury—of this there was no doubt. While some of the physicians felt a disc operation should be performed at once, others believed there was a chance of the injury healing without surgery. Finally, they agreed to wait a few months before making a decision.

The weeks that followed were agonizingly painful for Jack, but there was one redeeming feature. Since he could move around on crutches, he was given weekend passes from the hospital to visit his parents at Hyannis Port.

On the afternoon of August 12—just a year after the ramming of PT 109—Jack and Mr. and Mrs. Kennedy were seated in the huge living room of the Hyannis Port house. They discussed Kick's recent marriage to William Cavendish and read one of Joe's breezy letters from England where he was flying a Navy Liberator on antisubmarine patrol. Then a servant announced that two priests had arrived to see the Ambassador. Mr. Kennedy went out to speak to the clergymen privately. A few minutes later he returned, visibly shaken.

Joe had been reported missing in action, he announced ashen-faced.

The details the priests had given were sketchy, but ominous enough. Young Joe, who had asked to remain in combat although he had completed the required number of missions, had volunteered for a hazardous assignment. He was to pilot a bomber loaded with explosives to destroy the base of the V-2 rockets which the Nazis were using against London. Joe and his copilot were to set the controls to aim their plane at the V-2 launching site on the Belgian coast, then parachute to safety. From that point on, the ammunition plane was supposed to have been guided by remote control to the target. For some mysterious reason the bomber had blown up in mid-air just before leaving the English coast, and neither Joe nor his copilot had been found.

For the first few days, the family held out hope that the miracle of the previous year would be repeated and Joe would turn up alive. But as time passed and there was no word, they had to accept the tragic fact that he had been killed. The terrible finality of his older brother's death was hard on Jack, and he was grateful that Kick had flown in from England to be with the family in that difficult hour.

A month after Kick arrived at Hyannis Port, she received a cablegram from the British War Office. Her young bridegroom of four months had been killed in action while leading an infantry charge in France.

This news, coming so soon after Joe's death, was almost too much for the family to bear. Deep gloom, verging on despair, hung over the Kennedy household. Kick, in virtual shock, made ready to fly back to England to be with her husband's family.

Of the entire family, it was Rose Kennedy who, because of her deep religious faith, managed to bear up with the greatest stoicism. She helped bolster her husband and children with a spiritual strength that was towering.

During the next few months, Jack's life was one of constant mental and physical anguish. His injury had grown so painful that he was almost immobilized. Finally the doctors decided to perform the disc operation on his back.

He underwent surgery at the Chelsea Naval Hospital in the late fall. Recuperation was slow and painful. During convalescence his father suggested that he edit a book honoring Joe's memory. It was to be a volume of reminiscences by members of the family and friends and was to be privately published by the Kennedy family under the title, *As We Remember Joe*.

For Jack the chance to work was a godsend. Not only did it help take his mind off his physical discomfort, but it also served as an outlet for the guilt feelings that came from recollection of his childhood resentment of Joe.

In addition to editing the volume, he wrote a simple but moving little tribute to his dead older brother:

It is the realization that the future held the promise of great accomplishment for Joe that has made his death so particularly hard for those who knew him. His worldly success was so assured that his death seems to have cut into the natural order of things.

But at the same time there is a completeness to Joe's life, and that is the completeness of perfection. His life as he lived, and finally as he died, could hardly have been improved upon. And through it all, he had a deep and abiding faith— he was never far from God—and so I cannot help but feel that "Death to him was less a setting forth than a returning."

Early in 1945 Jack was discharged from the hospital. Thin and ailing, he went down to Washington to appear before a Navy board to determine whether he was physically fit to remain in the service. After examining the various medical reports, the board regretfully informed him that he would have to be retired from the Navy. Although he had tried to prepare himself for such news, he returned to civilian life disappointed, uncertain about the future and tormented by self-doubt as to his own capabilities.

On the front pages of the newspapers at this time, side by side with the war news, were announcements of an international conference to be held in San Francisco, beginning on April 25. It was to be attended by representatives of all the countries that were at war with Germany or Japan, as well as those which had been liberated. The aim was to fashion a "United Nations Organization" to deal with disputes between nations and provide for collective security against countries guilty of aggression.

Jack was intrigued by the coming conference and mentioned his interest to his father. As usual, the Ambassador came up with a practical suggestion. Would Jack like to cover it as a newspaperman? If so, he would put a call through to his old friend, newspaper publisher William Randolph Hearst.

In April Jack went to San Francisco as special correspondent for the *New York Journal-American* and other Hearst newspapers. His task was to report the events "from a GI viewpoint."

A press card, Jack soon learned, served as an admission ticket to a fascinating world of diplomatic intrigue, a world he had been too young to comprehend fully during his father's service as Ambassador to Britain.

Observing the conference at close quarters, he saw that in spite of a global war, national passions and selfishness still persisted. He even heard some delegates talking blithely "of fighting the Russians in the next ten or fifteen years." He came to realize that the achievement of mutual understanding and lasting peace would take time and patience. There was no simple overnight panacea to the complex problems of history, geography and economics that made for international hatred and distrust.

Jack wrote of these things in his dispatches. His sober, realistic appraisals and his conscientious effort to be accurate in his reporting earned him praise from the Hearst editors, even though his writing style was somewhat scholarly. The articles were published all over the country.

The deliberations at the San Francisco meeting included a great deal of wrangling, but in the end the delegates produced a charter for an international body dedicated to peace. On June 26, 1945, the representatives of fifty nations affixed their signatures to the document. With the signing of this charter, the "United Nations" was born.

So pleased were the Hearst executives with Jack's work that they asked him to take other assignments. The pain in his back had subsided since his discharge from the hospital so he accepted readily. By late spring of 1945, the war in Europe was over. A conference was called in Potsdam, Germany, by the victorious allies. Here, President Harry S. Truman, Prime Minister Winston Churchill and Premier Joseph Stalin were to meet to make postwar plans. Jack went to the Potsdam Conference. And from there he was sent to London to report on the British elections.

He wrote his stories in a sober, straightforward style. As a reporter he worked hard and was not content merely to rewrite official "handouts" or press releases, as some newspapermen were prone to do. Yet as the weeks passed, he gradually came to the conclusion that journalism was not for him. As an observer, a newspaperman was supposed to report what was happening, not make things happen. For this reason Jack felt that a journalist's life was too passive to suit him. For someone as restless as he, it would prove frustrating in the long run. So at twenty-eight he once again found himself groping for self-understanding, for a goal to give his life meaning.

It was his old Grandpa Fitz—Honey Fitz—still spry at eighty-two, who came forward with the suggestion that was to alter the course of Jack's existence.

In the summer of 1945, the United States Representative from Massachusetts' Eleventh District was James Michael Curley, a colorful old-line politician. Curley, like Honey Fitz, had spent his life in Boston politics and had served as mayor of Boston. Yet in spite of the similarity of backgrounds, personalities and careers, Curley and Honey Fitz had been lifelong political enemies.

Congressman Curley was not happy in his unfamiliar Washington surroundings. He felt homesick for his old political haunts in East Boston. So in November of

1945, he ran once again for mayor of Boston and won easily.

The departure of Curley from the House of Representatives left a congressional vacancy in the Eleventh District. It was at this point that Grandpa Fitz came up with a fantastic suggestion. Why not have Jack run for the unoccupied seat?

The notion was so absurd that Jack refused to entertain it. Unlike his brother Joe, he could never enjoy the rough and tumble of politics. Besides, he was no politician. The thought of introducing himself to people he didn't even know and asking them to vote for him was terrifying. He most certainly would feel embarrassed and apologetic, hardly the proper pose for an office-seeker hoping to project a picture of competence and self-assurance. Why, at Harvard he had not even been able to get himself elected president of his class!

Grandpa Fitz was not one to give up easily. Besides, he now had an ally in Jack's father. Although a year had passed since the news of Joe's passing, Mr. Kennedy was still in a state of deep despair. It seemed that with his oldest son's death the fundamental reason for his existence had died, too. Yet the suggestion that Jack run for Congress had a curious effect. Overnight some of the Ambassador's old sparkle seemed to return, and he gradually began to reach out into the mainstream of living once more.

He talked to Jack earnestly, almost pleadingly. Joe was to have entered politics but now Joe was gone. It would be good to have someone carry the Kennedy banner into the political fray. Indeed, it would be the best way he knew to honor Joe's memory.

Jack did not know what to do. His father's words had shaken his original resolve. When he protested that he was an amateur at politics and would not even know how to go about getting votes, Mr. Kennedy explained that it would be a family enterprise—the whole Kennedy clan would help him, including that professional of professionals, Grandpa Fitz. And since the Eleventh District was overwhelmingly Democratic, it was only a matter of campaigning hard until the primaries in June. Whoever won the primary designation as Democratic candidate would almost automatically win the seat in the November election.

Jack raised another objection: since he had no political background, why in the world should anyone want to vote for him? The Ambassador's reply was candidly to the point. He was a Kennedy and a Fitzgerald, wasn't he? With names like those, how could he lose in Boston? Besides, his reputation as a wartime hero would not hurt. Now that World War II was over, there was a great clamor throughout the country to give the veterans some voice in the policies of the nation they had helped save.

Jack finally agreed to run because he knew how much it meant to his father rather than out of any real political aspirations of his own. Once he said yes, he pitched headlong into the campaign. He was skinny and frighteningly underweight and his skin was still yellow from antimalarial drugs, but he did not spare himself. From morning to night he was on the go, holding strategy meetings, organizing campaign workers, ringing doorbells.

As his legal Boston residence, he used a hotel suite which the Kennedys maintained at the Bellevue Hotel, near the Statehouse. But as the campaign grew more hectic, he rented a three-room apartment where he met privately with campaign aides and caught a few hours of sleep away from the clamor of telephones and mimeograph machines.

In some respects, the primary campaign had the hilarious features of a three-ring circus. There were *nine* candidates for the Democratic nomination, including a former WAC major who campaigned in her military uniform and *two* candidates with the name of Joseph Russo!

Jack managed to organize an effective campaign. He called on his old friends from Choate, Harvard and the Navy for help, and they came to Boston to pitch in as campaign workers: Les Billings from Baltimore, Paul Fay from San Francisco and Torby Macdonald from Massachusetts. One of the most effective campaigners of all was Grandpa Fitz who used all of his Irish charm to persuade the people of East Boston to vote for his grandson.

At the start, one of the biggest obstacles was Jack's shyness. Withdrawn, full of self-doubt, apologetic even, he found it difficult to play the politician. Sometimes, just before having to face a group of voters, he would mumble in embarrassment to a close friend, "If Joe were alive, I wouldn't be in this. I'm only trying to fill his shoes."

But as the weeks passed, he forced himself to do what did not come naturally. Day after day, he went through the district, ringing doorbells, introducing himself, chatting with the residents. He made the rounds of taverns, garages, barbershops, piers and meeting halls. Fortunately, his back was holding up well in spite of the physical exertion required. As the campaign progressed, some of his old fears began to disappear, and he developed poise and self-confidence.

Indeed, he began to enjoy certain aspects of campaigning—particularly the spirit of competition.

Jack dealt with a variety of issues. On domestic matters, he followed a liberal Democratic program, backing veterans' benefits, social security, improved housing, rent controls and price controls. But he took care not to venture too deeply into foreign affairs, for he knew that the people of the Eleventh District were more interested in basic bread-and-butter issues than in international policy. He talked with them about their immediate problems and hopes, and left the larger issues to his opponents in the primary. Even his father was amazed at how quickly he had caught on to the art of political campaigning. "I never thought Jack had it in him," Mr. Kennedy confided to his friends.

For the Ambassador the campaign served as an emotional tonic. He poured money into the primary race as if it were a presidential election. But in spite of expensive brochures, newspaper advertisements and other publicity devices, Jack and his aides felt that something more personal was needed to reach the voters of the Eleventh District.

They soon found the answer: house parties! Jack's sisters and Mrs. Kennedy helped organize them. Campaign workers in every neighborhood were asked to throw open their homes to their neighbors. The Kennedy campaign organization provided dishes, cookies, coffee, tea and sandwiches. A careful record was kept of those who attended the parties, and later they were asked to talk to *their* neighbors on behalf of Jack's candidacy.

As the campaign drew to a close, a gigantic house party was held in a hotel. More than two thousand women voters were invited to have tea with Mr. and Mrs. Kennedy.

Primary night arrived at last. Jack went to the polls with his Grandpa and Grandma Fitz. They insisted on remaining at campaign headquarters while he went to a movie to relax. Afterward, he returned to headquarters and was greeted by cheering workers. The returns already in showed him to be far in the lead of any of the other candidates. When the entire vote was tabulated in the early morning hours, Jack's total amounted to 22,183, double that of his closest rival.

It was a stirring triumph, one which so overwhelmed eighty-three-year-old Grandpa Fitz that he climbed up on a table and happily danced a jig while singing "Sweet Adeline."

Four months later, on Election Day, Jack was formally elected Representative of the Eleventh District of Massachusetts. Shortly afterward, he went down to Washington to prepare to take up his duties as a United States congressman.

He rented a house in the lovely old Georgetown section of the capital. Since his sister Eunice was doing social service work in Washington, it was agreed that she would share the house with him. Margaret Ambrose, a Kennedy family retainer for years, was sent to Washington by Mrs. Kennedy to serve as Jack's housekeeper, with orders to fatten him up.

In Washington, his thin frame and boyish features presented something of a problem. Soon a story began making the rounds that when Jack first tried to enter the House Chamber, the guards had mistaken him for a congressional page boy! Another time he slipped into a pair of slacks and sweat shirt and joined football practice at a local high school where he had gotten to know the coach. A short time later, the coach came out on the football field and approached the halfback. "How's the Congressman doing?" he asked. "Oh, is that what they call that tall, skinny kid?" the lad retorted. "He sure needs a lot of practice."

Tourists who saw Jack flitting about Capitol Hill rarely guessed that he was a Congressman, and he made no effort to fit the part. A careless dresser even in the Navy, he did not bother to change his habits in civilian life. Occasionally, he would show up on the floor of the House Chamber wearing a shirt, tie and jacket over khaki trousers left over from his service days!

As a young, handsome and unmarried Congressman, Jack found life pleasant enough in Washington. As a freshman legislator he was not on any important congressional committees, so his responsibilities were not onerous. There was time to play golf, swim or fly to Hyannis Port or Palm Beach to visit his family. In the evenings and on weekends, he dated many of the attractive girls in the capital.

Yet he did not neglect his political tasks. He had been told by his Grandpa Fitz that the first duty of a politician was to his constituents—those who had voted him into office. To make certain that they would vote for him again, he opened up headquarters in the Post Office Building in Boston, in addition to his official office in the Capitol. He staffed it with bright, efficient clerks who handled the individual problems of his constituents intelligently and quickly.

If a family was planning to vacation in Washington and wanted passes for a House session, Representative Kennedy's office could arrange it. A complaint of bureaucratic treatment by a government agency would get quicker response if filed through the young Congressman's office. Did Professor Jones at Harvard want to receive the *Congressional Record* regularly? Mr. Kennedy would be glad to take care of it.

These were routine political chores, but they meant votes. Furthermore, for the youthful Congressman it was an invaluable education in the everyday problems of people.

Because of his lack of seniority, Jack sponsored no important legislation himself, but he did back the measures he had promised to support during his campaign. Since housing was in desperately short supply, particularly for veterans, he was a strong proponent of housing bills that would step up construction of low and middle income housing, and he fought moves to weaken rent controls. He opposed attempts to cut down on the school lunch program of the federal government and voted against a tax bill that would have helped the wealthy oil industry at the expense of the small taxpayer. On all of these issues he reflected the viewpoint of those who had voted for him, convinced that it was his duty as an elected official to represent the opinions of the electorate. On foreign affairs, however, he took no strong stand of his own.

Kennedy continued to keep his aspirations clearly in mind at all times. True, he had originally resisted the notion of becoming a politician. But having entered politics, he was now determined to try with all his might to succeed at it. And since he was just now learning his profession, he felt he had no time to philosophize or reflect on the subtleties of political theory, as he had learned them in Professor Holcombe's class at Harvard. For the moment, he was content to measure his success as a politician by the number of votes he was able to win.

Indeed, he was so busy attending to the needs of his constituents in Boston that he was often away from Washington. But on the issues that were important to his people, he was always present to make himself heard, so that as far as the voters of the Eleventh District were concerned, Representative Kennedy could do no wrong.

Many of the Democratic ward bosses in Boston resented him. They felt he was a "Johnny-come-lately" to politics who had won the office because of his family name and his father's money. They disliked him because he could afford the luxury of political independence which many other officeholders did not enjoy. He was no Democratic "wheelhorse" who had come up through the ranks and owed his nomination to some political boss. He had run his own campaign with the help of family and friends. Consequently, his concern was catering to the voters, not the ward bosses, and he rejected the attempts of the politicians to intervene for jobs and favors on their behalf.

For Kennedy, those early years in Congress served as a political apprenticeship. He improved his public speaking style, his ability to deal easily with people, his knowledge of political techniques. His former reluctance to introduce himself to strangers or to talk before groups was now a thing of the past. By the time 1948 arrived, he was beginning to develop the self-confidence and poise of the professional politician. Furthermore, he was so secure in his district that there were strong rumors that no one would even dare run against him in the primaries that year, so that his reelection to the House of Representatives was assured.

Kennedy's relations with his fellow legislators were excellent. He was popular and well liked even among the Republicans, in spite of political differences. It was not unusual for him to engage a fellow legislator in vehement floor debate in the afternoon, then go out with him on a double date in the evening. Although he had a wide circle of friends in Congress, he was closest to George Smathers of Florida who, like him, was a freshman in the House of Representatives and a bachelor.

To Kennedy, the thought of remaining a member of the House permanently was not appealing. Since he had given himself to politics, he wanted to go as far and as fast as he could in his chosen field. Therefore, he began to look around for possible avenues of advancement.

As a Representative there were two offices to which he could reasonably aspire: the governorship of Massachusetts or a Senate seat. Since his re-election to the House was virtually guaranteed, he saw no reason why he should not begin at once to make a name for himself on a statewide basis, in anticipation of that future time when one of these two offices would open up.

Therefore, throughout the winter and spring of 1948, instead of campaigning in his own Eleventh District, Kennedy spent his time speaking before civic groups and clubs in every corner of Massachusetts. He also had friends and aides tour the state to collect lists of local leaders—businessmen, civic officers and outstanding private citizens—who might be interested in assisting in a Kennedy campaign for some unknown office at some unknown time in the future!

Among his helpers were two young men, Kenneth O'Donnell and Lawrence F. O'Brien. O'Donnell, a dark, lean youth, was a close friend of Kennedy's younger brother, Bobby, who was now attending law school at the University of Virginia. Bobby and Kenny O'Donnell had been on the Harvard football team together. O'Brien, stocky, with a placid, round face, had served as secretary to another Massachusetts congressman, Foster Furcolo. He had been recommended to Jack because of his experience in grass roots political organization. Together, O'Donnell and O'Brien formed a shrewd, hard-working political team. They used the lists of leading citizens to organize Kennedy committees throughout the state. These committees, in turn, exerted their influence to get additional speaking engagements for their candidate. There were many nights when Kennedy, accompanied by a friend or two, ignored weather warnings to brave the icy winter roads of the Berkshire Mountains in order to fulfill a speaking commitment before a businessmen's group or parent-teachers association.

By the time spring arrived, Kennedy was satisfied that he had made a good start. His face and voice were now known throughout Massachusetts. Even the oldline political leaders who resented this young upstart had to admit that he was doing an effective job of getting himself publicized.

Early in May, Kennedy's efforts to advance his political career were suddenly interrupted by tragic news from Europe. His father was in Paris and on his way to a brief vacation on the Riviera. Kick, who had been living in England since the death of her husband four years earlier, decided to visit the Ambassador in France. A friend of hers, a young English nobleman, had chartered a small plane to fly to Cannes and invited her to go along. She accepted the offer. Flying at night, the plane was caught in rain and fog. The pilot lost his bearings and crashed into the Ardèche Mountains in southern France. Everyone was killed. Joseph P. Kennedy was called out at night to identify his daughter's body.

The news of Kathleen's death left Jack in a state of shock. Of all his brothers and sisters he had felt closest to her. He found it almost impossible to accept the fact of her death, just as he had had difficulty accepting the reality of Joe's death. For many weeks his political career was all but forgotten as he sought to extricate himself from the cloud of depression which enveloped him.

Once again it was Rose Kennedy's spiritual strength and philosophical acceptance of God's will which bolstered the other members of the family in their time of sorrow.

Slowly, Kennedy began to pick up the threads of his life. He resumed his statewide campaigning in the hope that hard work would prove an effective antidote to despair. By late spring he had made such an impact that there was already talk of running him for state-wide office in the future. That June he won the Democratic primary without opposition, thus assuring his re-election to the House of Representatives.

9

JACQUELINE

Kennedy's second term as Congressman was almost a replica of the first. He continued to preoccupy himself with bread-and-butter domestic legislation while trying to avoid involvement in the bitter foreign policy wrangles taking place. Yet with winds of change blowing across the world, there were times when he had to take a stand on international matters. These winds had chilled relations between the West and the Communist world, thus bringing about a "cold war" situation. All across America people were concerned with the threat of new hostilities.

Three years before, in August of 1945, an American B-29 had dropped the first atom bomb over Japan. The explosion had ended the war and changed the world for all time. Now, in the wake of the bitter antagonism between East and West, a new terror was stalking the earth: the fear of atomic war. While the United States alone had atom bombs, there was little doubt that in the future the Soviet Union would develop similar weapons.

In Boston, where the Roman Catholic population was large, hatred of Communists ran deep, for the people considered them adherents of a godless philosophy intent on destroying the world. Some of Kennedy's more violent constituents actually advocated declaring war on Russia "to destroy them before they destroy us!" A great many more felt that the United States should maintain strong military defenses while adhering to a policy of semi-isolationism. Among the champions of this latter view was the Ambassador, for whom this was a natural evolvement of his prewar position.

Congressman Kennedy found himself torn between the need to represent his constituents and the knowledge that foreign issues often were too complex to be solved by such simple formulas. As a result, he was unable to devise a consistent approach to foreign policy, and his voting record reflected this fact.

But in spite of his own internal conflicts on some issues, he was entirely consistent in his approach to his own political future. He was out to make a name for himself, and he was determined to spare no effort toward this goal. Accordingly, he flew up to Massachusetts almost every weekend to take part in a whirlwind round of speeches, visits and conferences at women's clubs, schools and veterans' meetings. His meals were eaten on the run. Often they consisted of little more than a hamburger and milk shake or a bowl of hot tomato soup, with a chocolate bar for dessert. On Sunday nights he returned to Washington and his legislative duties.

The year 1950 was a significant one. It marked Kennedy's re-election to a third term in the House. But it also saw the death of Grandpa Fitz at the age of eighty-seven. And in June of that year, the cold war which had held the world in a paralyzing vise for almost five years suddenly turned hot in a remote corner of the world called Korea.

Korea was an ancient and unhappy land. Enslaved by Japan in 1910, she had been liberated after World War II and occupied by the Soviet Union in the north and United States troops in the south. In 1948, this temporary occupation had formed the basis for creating two separate countries—a Communist North Korea and a Republican South Korea, with the dividing line set at the 38th parallel of latitude.

After two years of strained relations between the two governments which were reflected in frequent boundary skirmishes, Communist North Korean forces crossed the border into South Korea on June 25, 1950. On learning the news, President Harry Truman immediately announced that the United States would help repel the invasion with planes and troops, for he was convinced that this was a critical test of the democratic world's fortitude in dealing with Communist aggression. He also called on the United Nations to join in giving military aid to the nation under attack.

A resolution was adopted by the Security Council of the UN, calling on all member nations to oppose the aggressors with force. The motion passed only because the Soviet representative on the Security Council who could have vetoed it happened to be boycotting the Council's meetings at the time!

Member countries all over the world began to pour troops and arms into Korea to beat back the attackers in the world's first "police action" against a lawless nation. The fighting in Korea soon settled into a bloody drawn-out struggle. "Volunteers" from Communist China began "enlisting" in droves in the North Korean forces.

In America, the Korean police action was not a popular war. Many did not understand the principle of collective security which required that the United States pledge the lives and fortunes of Americans to safeguard a remote country in Asia from aggression.

Congressman Kennedy's mail reflected some of the public's frustration with the Korean police action. He himself expressed criticism of President Truman's strong stand in Korea, arguing that the use of American troops there would mean a weakening of democratic defenses in western Europe.

In June of 1951, in the midst of these policy debates, Jack's attention was temporarily diverted by another interest—a radiantly beautiful young lady named Jacqueline Lee Bouvier. They met at a dinner party in the home of Charles Bartlett, a Washington correspondent for *The Chattanooga Times*. The Bartletts had been scheming for weeks to get Miss Bouvier, twenty-two, and the handsome, eligible thirty-four-year-old bachelor together. Jacqueline—everyone called her "Jackie" —was in the senior class at George Washington University. She was a tall, slim, dark-haired beauty with a soft voice and feminine ways.

When the party was over, Jack escorted the girl to her car and was about to ask her for a date when he was startled to see a young man sitting in the vehicle. Jackie also appeared surprised, but Jack did not wait for an explanation. He hurriedly bade her good night and left. It was the last he was to see of her for many months.

Jacqueline Lee Bouvier was descended from two of New York's most socially prominent families. Her mother was the former Janet Lee, daughter of a New York banker, and her father was John Vernon Bouvier

III, a stockbroker who traced his ancestry back to a French soldier who had fought under Washington in the Revolution.

Jackie had been brought up according to the prescribed code of high society. She and her younger sister, Lee, had attended the best private schools and received every luxury money could buy. But in spite of wealth and social status, Jackie's childhood had not been wholly happy. When she was ten, her mother and father were divorced. Two years later, Mrs. Bouvier married Hugh D. Auchincloss, a member of the New York Stock Exchange. Jackie's new stepfather had two sons and a daughter of his own by a previous marriage.

After attending an exclusive finishing school, Jackie went to Vassar for two years, then spent a year in Paris where she studied art, music and poetry. After returning to the United States she decided to complete her college education at George Washington University, in Washington, D.C.

Miss Bouvier's brief encounter with Jack Kennedy at the home of the Charles Bartletts did not leave a favorable impression on her. In fact her reaction was one of mild annoyance at the young Congressman's failure to give her an opportunity to explain the presence of the man he had seen in the car. Actually, the story was innocent enough. The youth was one of several who had been dating her in recent weeks. That particular evening he had been walking along a quiet Georgetown street when he noticed her automobile at the curb. He thereupon had taken the liberty of sitting in the car to wait for her to come out, so he could see her.

A short time later, Miss Bouvier took a leave of absence from school to take a job on *The Washington*

Times-Herald as the newspaper's "Inquiring Camera Girl," and she almost forgot Congressman Jack Kennedy. Her job was to interview prominent Washingtonians for their views on various issues. Although she scarcely knew a lens from a shutter, the male photographers were so smitten with her wide eyed beauty that they fell over themselves trying to help her.

In the late winter of 1952, the capital was alive with rumors that a political bombshell was about to be dropped in Massachusetts. According to reports, the incumbent Senator Henry Cabot Lodge, a veteran Republican campaigner, would be opposed in the coming election by young Congressman Kennedy! Miss Bouvier was ordered by her editor to interview Jack.

Recalling his behavior on the night of the Bartletts' dinner party, she was not too enthused by the assignment. Nevertheless, she called him for an appointment, trying to sound briskly professional. He recognized her at once. During the interview he confessed sheepishly that since the evening of the dinner party he had never been able to get her out of his mind, and he grinned in embarrassment at his own stupidity when she explained why the young man had been sitting in her car during the Bartletts' party. He asked her for a date and she accepted. Soon they were going out together regularly —to movies, concerts and parties.

As the race for the Senate grew hotter, Kennedy's campaigning took him to Massachusetts for longer and longer periods of time. Sometimes he would take a few hours off to fly down to Washington to see Jackie; but most often they talked by long-distance telephone, to the accompaniment of a loud clinking of coins.

When Kennedy had first announced his candidacy, most political observers—even a number of his friends

—were convinced that he was out of his mind. Henry Cabot Lodge, Jr. came from one of Massachusetts' most distinguished families. His father had been a Senator, and he himself had earned a phenomenal record over the years as a successful political campaigner. He was handsome, popular and attractive to women voters.

But Kennedy knew something the doubters didn't know: during the past few years he had campaigned in almost every one of Massachusetts' three hundred and fifty-one cities and towns. So that while he was only a Representative, his name and face and voice were now known throughout the state. Furthermore, he had a well-organized army of campaign workers operating on his behalf. True, they were "amateurs" in the sense that they had not been active in party politics before; but they were an enthusiastic group—young in age and spirit—who would make up in energy and determination what they lacked in experience.

In choosing his campaign manager Kennedy again astounded the professional politicians by selecting his younger brother, Bobby. Only twenty-seven, Bobby was fresh out of the University of Virginia Law School and recently married to the former Ethel Skakel, a college roommate of his sister Jean's. Since he had no background at all in Massachusetts politics, Bobby indeed seemed like the world's worst choice; but Jack had absolute faith in his brother's intelligence, astuteness and capacity to learn. Besides, there were Kenny O'Donnell and Larry O'Brien to help him out.

The skeptics shook their heads. "I don't know where he gets them but they're all *new,*" one veteran of Massachusetts' political wars told a reporter. "Guys who have been in politics here for years don't know any of them."

But if the politicians did not know the Kennedy people, many of Jack's aides did not know the politicians either. One day a very prominent local political boss called at the Kennedy campaign headquarters. He was dumbfounded to learn that no one present, not even Bobby Kennedy, recognized his face or name.

"You mean to say nobody here knows me," he exclaimed derisively. "And you call *this* a political headquarters." Annoyed by the man's abusive tone and language, quick-tempered Bobby ordered him to leave.

The campaign followed the pattern of Kennedy's first hectic race for the House seat six years before. All the members of his family threw themselves into the campaign as did Torby Macdonald and his other friends. The Kennedy girls and Mrs. Kennedy were hostesses at innumerable coffee and tea parties. In addition, Mrs. Kennedy agreed to deliver a series of campaign speeches before groups of women voters.

As the beautiful mother of two war heroes—one dead and the other a Congressman—as well as the wife of a former Ambassador, she made the ideal campaigner. On each occasion she managed to establish an immediate rapport with the group she was addressing. In the North End of Boston she greeted those of Italian descent with a few words in Italian and told them how she had grown up in their neighborhood. When addressing crowds of housewives, she showed them the index cards she had used to keep track of her children's vaccinations and medical treatments. At a gathering of society women she would talk briefly about her son's candidacy, then pause and say, "Now let me tell you about the new dresses I saw last month." Long before

Election Day, it became apparent that Mrs. Kennedy was one of the sensations of the campaign.

For Kennedy himself the race was an exhausting ordeal. He spoke and traveled and conferred constantly, living on an occasional hamburger and milk shake and grabbing off a few hours of sleep when he could. The constant physical strain was also causing his back trouble to act up again, for the first time in a long while. As the campaign progressed, the pain became so acute that he had to walk on crutches most of the time. But when the time came to walk down an aisle to a speaker's rostrum, he handed the crutches to Torby Macdonald or some other friend and marched up to the platform as straight as an arrow, in spite of the excruciating pain.

In his choice of campaign issues, Kennedy followed the pattern of his earlier congressional campaigns. He concentrated on local and state issues and played down international problems. He felt there were good reasons for doing so. His own advisers were split on what course to follow. Those who represented labor unions and other liberal support urged him to base his campaign on a liberal, internationalist platform. Other advisers, notably his own father, still adhered to their semi-isolationist views and tried to persuade him to attack Henry Cabot Lodge as an interventionist who favored bleeding the United States on behalf of undeserving foreign governments. When bitter wrangling broke out between the two factions in his own organization, Kennedy decided to settle the dispute by avoiding the issue.

He faced a similar dilemma over another, even more delicate, problem. For several years, a Wisconsin Senator named Joe McCarthy had been successfully exploiting American fear of communism by leveling charges of "communism and treason" against many government officials. He had inspired such a climate of terror and suspicion as a result of his public attacks on those with whom he disagreed that his tactics had won the name of "McCarthyism."

Jack disliked McCarthy. He considered the Wisconsin Senator crude, boorish and deceitful. Yet McCarthy was politically powerful, for he had persuaded many Americans that he was leading an effective crusade against communism. He was especially popular in Boston, where there was strong pro-McCarthy sentiment among the Irish Catholics. In fact, Mr. Kennedy had once contributed money to McCarthy's election campaign.

As in the case of the foreign policy dilemma, Kennedy decided to resolve the McCarthy issue by acting as if it did not exist. Lodge did the same. The result was a curiously provincial campaign by each candidate as to who could help the state of Massachusetts more.

"Kennedy will do *more* for Massachusetts," read the billboards and posters prepared by Jack's aides.

"Lodge has done—and will do—the *Most* for Massachusetts," shrieked his opponent's placards.

In spite of its local flavor, the Kennedy-Lodge battle was being waged against the backdrop of an exciting presidential campaign. General Dwight D. Eisenhower had been nominated to run on the Republican ticket, while the Democrats had chosen former Governor Adlai E. Stevenson of Illinois, a graceful, polished man who was a master of elegant prose. Kennedy greatly admired Stevenson and gave his candidacy strong support in Massachusetts, but it was obvious that Eisenhower, because of his record as America's leading war hero, was the popular favorite.

Kennedy knew that if Eisenhower won nationally, he would draw many independent votes in Massachusetts into the Republican column. Furthermore, Massachusetts' other Senator, Leverett Saltonstall, a Republican, was campaigning for Lodge. Consequently, Kennedy was convinced that he must run "scared." He felt that if his own campaign faltered even briefly, it could prove his political undoing. Therefore, he continued to campaign at such a pitch that many weary aides could not help wondering whether they would last until the election.

Finally November arrived. The arguments and debates and rallies were over. Now the people went to the polls to make their choice. On election night, Kennedy sat in his campaign headquarters with Bobby and the others to await the returns. He felt tense but unworried. He wryly wondered whether the campaign had taken so much out of him that he no longer had the capacity to care about the outcome.

By early morning it was clear that Eisenhower had beaten Stevenson by a huge margin. Lodge was ahead of Kennedy, but by a much smaller margin, and there were still critical areas to be heard from. These were hopeful signs. Yet many of Kennedy's campaign workers were despondent.

The candidate himself was untroubled. So convinced was he of ultimate victory that he turned to Torby Macdonald and mused, "I wonder what job Eisenhower's going to give Lodge."

Suddenly, the vote on the tally boards was beginning to change. Kennedy slowly began to edge up on his opponent. Then he was ahead. A few of the campaign workers cheered wearily. At six in the morning Henry Cabot Lodge conceded.

Kennedy had won the election by a margin of seventy thousand votes. So spectacular was his triumph in the face of the national ticket's defeat that he found himself the dominant political figure in the state of Massachusetts.

The excitement of the election campaign had barely ebbed when Kennedy undertook a different kind of campaign—the renewal of his romance with Jacqueline Bouvier. To make up for lost time, he dated her several times a week. Instead of flowers and candy he presented her with history books and biographies.

Meanwhile, Miss Bouvier continued to work at her job on the *Times-Herald*. Early in 1953 she was sent to London to cover the coronation of Queen Elizabeth II from the "woman's angle." In spite of his back trouble, Kennedy saw her off at the airport. In London she received a cablegram from him. "Articles excellent," the message read, "but you are missed."

When she returned she found Kennedy waiting at the unloading gate as she stepped down from her plane. He proposed then and there and she accepted.

During the following months she got a foretaste of what it would mean to be married to a Kennedy. On a visit to Hyannis Port, she was astounded at the size of the family. And she was also amazed to discover that the favorite pastime was playing touch football, a strenuous activity in which everybody—husbands, wives and children—participated with an appalling enthusiasm. Relentlessly they swam, played tennis and went sailing. Even Jack would strap up his back in order to participate!

Jackie, who didn't know a pass from a punt, began

121

to wonder what she had gotten herself into. She had supposed that she was marrying Jack Kennedy, only to learn that she was joining a football team. Nevertheless, she took it like a good sport.

On September 12, 1953, Senator John Fitzgerald Kennedy, thirty-six, and Jacqueline Lee Bouvier, twenty-four, were married in St. Mary's Roman Catholic Church in Newport, Rhode Island. Since the bride was also a Roman Catholic, there was no religious problem to face. Richard Cardinal Cushing of Boston, an old friend of the Ambassador's, officiated at the wedding.

It was one of the year's outstanding social events. More than three thousand persons gathered outside the cathedral to catch a glimpse of the couple. Afterward a reception for eight hundred guests was held at nearby Hammersmith Farm, which was owned by the bride's stepfather, Hugh Auchincloss. The groom's face was badly scratched and he had to explain to all who inquired how he had tumbled into a rose bush the previous day while playing touch football!

10

A TIME FOR COURAGE

Soon after their return from a honeymoon in Aca-
pulco, Mexico, the Kennedys rented a large rambling
house in nearby Virginia. For the youthful bride, the
task of decorating and furnishing their new home was
an artistic challenge, and she threw herself into it enthusiastically.

Once they were settled, they entertained friends and
their respective families with warmth and grace. Out-
wardly, their marriage seemed ideal. Yet in truth they
themselves sensed that their marriage was not going as
smoothly as they had dreamed.

All newlyweds encounter difficulty in adjustment at
first, but for Senator and Mrs. Kennedy the problem
was complicated by his political career. Life for a politician is continually hectic; for his wife it can be even
more so. Jackie discovered that marriage to a United
States Senator was a continuous round of banquets,
dedications and political meetings. In addition the
close-knit Kennedy clan had a tradition of almost
weekly family reunions that further reduced privacy.

The demands on Senator Kennedy's time were so
intense that the newlyweds were more apt to be in

Boston, Hyannis Port, New York or Palm Beach than at their own Virginia home. And of course Jackie was expected to participate in all of her husband's activities. On the few occasions when she was not with him, other politicians or members of the Kennedy clan raised eyebrows.

Another cause of marital tension was Senator Kennedy's back trouble. He had been in agonizing pain during portions of the senatorial race, but he had hoped that once the strain of campaigning was over, it would subside. It didn't. Soon he was entirely dependent on crutches, and the pain was so bad that it made him unusually irritable.

Moreover, the couple's divergent interests added still a third source of friction. Kennedy's total preoccupation with politics did not leave him much time for other activities. Despite his love of reading and his innate curiosity about literally everything, there was little opportunity for art, music and other cultural pastimes. Mrs. Kennedy, on the other hand, liked nothing better than to go to a concert or visit an art museum or relax in intellectual conversation at small, informal gatherings. Once she was asked by a newspaperman about her husband's preferences in music. She replied with quiet humor, "His favorite song is 'Hail to the Chief.'" Actually, Kennedy himself had a healthy respect for culture and the arts, but he felt that to take time out from politics at that particular phase of his career was a luxury he could ill afford.

As their first anniversary approached, Mrs. Kennedy learned that she was going to have a baby. They were overjoyed, but the couple's delight turned to ashes when complications developed and Jackie suffered a miscarriage. For both Senator and Mrs. Kennedy, it was many weeks before they emerged from the depression that engulfed them.

However, some good things were happening, too. The huge Kennedy clan now boasted two new faces. Kennedy's sisters Eunice and Patricia had recently married—Eunice to R. Sargent Shriver and Pat to Peter Lawford. Shriver, a member of an old Maryland family and a graduate of Yale Law School, had been working for Ambassador Kennedy as a manager of his vast real estate holdings. Lawford was a British-born Hollywood star with a keen sense of humor. When he was first introduced to his future father-in-law, the Ambassador told him pointedly, "If there's anything I think I'd hate as a son-in-law, it's an actor, and if there's anything I'd hate worse than an actor as a son-in-law it's an English actor." His future son-in-law nodded amiably and agreed that he had an excellent point.

There was still another new face on the scene—that of a young man named Theodore C. Sorensen. After his election to the Senate, Kennedy began to cast about for a competent aide—one who could help him draft speeches, compile legislative research and do other chores. Senator Paul Douglas of Illinois had suggested the youthful Sorensen who was twenty-four and a recent graduate of the University of Nebraska Law School. Tall, handsome and boyish-looking, Sorensen was the son of a maverick Republican attorney in Nebraska who had spent his life backing liberal causes. Ted Sorensen himself inherited from his father a liberal idealism which he tempered with a realistic approach to problems. Kennedy decided to hire the Nebraskan.

The choice turned out to be the right one. His new aide was well read, brilliant and incisive. As a speech writer he had a masterful gift for presenting ideas simply and elegantly. Indeed, Kennedy himself could not help but envy young Sorensen for the consistency of his liberalism and contrast it with his own patch-quilt political philosophy. Soon he found himself soliciting Ted Sorensen's views on a variety of subjects.

By the fall of 1954, Kennedy's back injury was so painful that he was desperate for any sort of relief. There had been a parade of physicians. Some had recommended more surgery—a long, delicate operation involving a double fusing of the spinal discs, which required the utmost skill. Others had advised against it, arguing that it might prove fatal, for they felt that his adrenal insufficiency would increase the chances of hemorrhage and infection.

In the end the decision had to be made by Kennedy himself. He stared down at his crutches and muttered defiantly, "I'd rather die than spend the rest of my life on these things."

On October 21, 1954, the lengthy operation was performed at the Hospital for Special Surgery in New York City. Afterward the patient was brought back to his room where he lay flat on his back, unable to sit up or move around.

During the next six weeks the pain continued without letup. Mrs. Kennedy was by his side at all times, reading aloud, handling telephone calls or telling jokes to try to raise his spirits. Finally, at Christmas, he was carried out of the hospital on a stretcher, and he and Jackie were flown down to Palm Beach where the rest of the Kennedy family was staying.

The sun was bright and warm and the weather was thoroughly delightful, but while his spirits improved, his back did not get any better. The following month he returned to New York for a second operation. So dismal were the prospects that a priest was called in and last rites were said before the patient was wheeled into the operating room. For hours the surgeons labored, while Mrs. Kennedy waited outside fearfully. When the operation was over, one of the surgeons came out and informed her that he thought everything would be all right. She uttered a silent prayer of thanks.

Once again Jackie was at her husband's side continually while he fought to recover. For Kennedy, the close brush with death had given him a curious feeling of humility, a desire to indulge in quiet introspection which he had not experienced since the war. He could recall the times prior to the sinking of PT 109 when he had wondered how he would react under pressure. In retrospect, he had no reason to be ashamed of his own performance.

Yet in his wartime reflections on the nature of courage, he had associated it primarily with physical bravery. Now, as he looked at his wife, who displayed a cheerfulness she did not feel in order to raise his morale, he could not help but wonder about moral courage that had nothing to do with physical danger. For the rest of his life he would always think of his wife as the embodiment of this kind of quiet heroism— a heroism he had first recognized in his mother during times of adversity. He knew then that in spite of earlier doubts, their marriage was as solid as two people who were deeply in love could make it.

During those endless days of convalescence, the issue of courage and its moral and philosophical implications continued to preoccupy Kennedy. Ernest Hemingway, he recalled, had defined it as "grace under pressure." It was a good definition. He liked it. It meant doing the right thing, no matter how compelling the reasons to do otherwise.

There must be room for courage in political life, too, he reasoned, though he had been too busy as a politician to give much thought to it in the past. Lying flat on his back and staring up at the ceiling, he wondered whether the subject of courage and politics would make an interesting book. There must be numerous instances of individual moral fortitude in American politics. Perhaps, if presented in a popular, dramatic style, these would appeal to lay readers. Once before he had given fleeting thought to the idea, but lack of time had kept him from doing much about it. Now, however, there was time to spare.

Kennedy had Jackie call up Ted Sorensen and ask him to come to the hospital. Sorensen agreed that a book such as Senator Kennedy described might be interesting and offered to begin doing research at once. Mrs. Kennedy, too, encouraged her husband to undertake the project, for she felt that if nothing else it would help him while away the weeks of prolonged idleness.

Among the instances of political courage which Sorensen dug up was the account of Governor Sam Houston's fight to keep Texas from seceding from the Union in 1861, even though his own constituents called him a traitor to Texas. Another was the dramatic story of Senator Edmund G. Ross who risked his political life to vote against the impeachment of President Andrew Jackson, over the violent protests of the voters who had elected him. And there was the heroic decision of Governor John Peter Altgeld of Illinois to pardon three men convicted of participating in the famous Haymarket Square bombing in Chicago, because he felt they had been unfairly tried and unjustly convicted. When a colleague asked if his action was politically wise, Altgeld had retorted, "It is right."

It was just such stories that Kennedy was eager to include in his book. His wife assisted by taking notes and helping to organize the manuscript. Sorensen served as a one-man research department and editorial board. He dug up material, reviewed Kennedy's drafts and checked the manuscript with leading historians to assure its accuracy. The Library of Congress sent over cartons of books. Kennedy wrote in longhand, setting down his stories on white sheets of paper. He frequently crossed out words and sentences, then made additions in the margins. The second draft was dictated from the rough copy to a secretary who then typed the pages of manuscript and sent it to Sorensen for criticism and suggestions.

Kennedy and Sorensen argued long and often about various points. So close was the collaboration that the two men soon were able to anticipate each other's thoughts and reactions. One of the central questions they discussed was the moral of the book. What should it all mean? Why did the men Kennedy was writing about defy their constituencies to perform their political acts of courage? In considering the answer, the author could not help recalling with a twinge of guilt his own failure to take a position on the McCarthy issue.

His initial impulse was to conclude that the heroes of his book had acted in the face of adverse public opinion because they felt that they were doing the right thing for their constituents, even though the people themselves did not realize it at the time. "They loved the public better than themselves" was the way he phrased it in the manuscript. But Sorensen insisted that this was not the whole story. It was the need to maintain one's self-respect that was the essential reason, he argued. Indeed, to Sam Houston, Edmund G. Ross, John Peter Altgeld and the others, conscience was more important than popularity or desire for political success.

Kennedy listened carefully—and realized that Sorensen was right. In the final analysis, the bulwark of democracy was faith in people. Democratic survival was based on the principle that the people elected men not merely to represent their views faithfully but to exercise conscientious judgment, even when it ran counter to popular opinion.

For Kennedy the writing of the book was not only a challenge but a political and personal catharsis. Although he had been in public office for almost eight years, he felt that for the first time he was on his way to formulating a consistent political philosophy. He realized that his earlier concept of a politician's responsibility to the voters had been a narrow, immature one. Courage was not restricted to physical heroism; it was also the moral strength to fight for a principle, to retain one's self-respect, even at the risk of certain defeat.

With the strengthening of the intellectual bonds between Kennedy and Sorensen and the maturing of the Senator's liberal philosophy came other insights. People like Sorensen, he now realized, had their liberalism "made" by the time they reached their late twenties. His own liberalism had bloomed late in the season, for it had been nurtured on a piecemeal basis, beginning with his father's advocacy of FDR's New Deal economic principles. However, now at last he felt that he possessed a consistent, unified political philosophy with which he could feel truly at ease.

A title was needed for the book. After considering and discarding dozens—some were suggested by Mrs. Kennedy and Sorensen and others—Senator Kennedy hit on a simple, dramatic title—*Profiles in Courage.* Everyone agreed that it was perfect. The book was to be dedicated to his wife.

The first publisher to whom the manuscript was submitted was Harper & Brothers. Fourteen years earlier Harper had rejected *Why England Slept,* but its editors did not make the same mistake again. Their reaction was immediate and favorable—and took the form of a book contract.

The only criticism by the editors was that the chapters, each dealing with an individual act of political courage, needed to be tied together. Accordingly, Kennedy agreed to write brief anecdotal introductions, setting the stage for each story by commenting on its significance. The foreword to the book was written by Allan Nevins, the eminent Columbia University historian to whom Ted Sorensen had submitted the manuscript for criticism, comment and verification of historical accuracy.

In spite of his long months of convalescence, Kennedy's back still bothered him. A distinguished woman physician, Dr. Janet Travell of New York, was finally called in. She began to treat him with sizable doses of Novocain which were injected into the muscle. Although this did not cure the condition, it relieved the pain so that for the first time in twelve years he could move about in relative comfort.

In late May of 1955, the Kennedys returned to Washington. The Senator was greeted with a standing ovation by the members of both parties in the Senate.

He was deeply moved by the genuine and spontaneous nature of the gesture.

The return to the capital plunged Kennedy once more into the midst of the political fray. During his long stay in the hospital, William Burke had begun to amass political power in Massachusetts. Burke resented the young Senator's popularity, and by getting himself elected state Democratic chairman he was threatening to undermine Kennedy's influence. He was also strongly opposed to the nomination of Adlai Stevenson as Democratic presidential candidate in the coming 1956 campaign and made it abundantly clear that he planned to hurt Stevenson's chances at the national convention which was eight months away.

Kennedy, a strong admirer of Stevenson's who was the leading presidential contender in spite of his 1952 defeat by Eisenhower, immediately devised strategy to fight Burke for control of the Democratic state committee in Massachusetts. He sent out word to all his supporters to do political battle. The doorbells in Massachusetts rang once more as registered members of the Democratic party were approached and asked to swing their weight behind Kennedy. The campaign was so effective that when the intraparty war was over, Burke was out and Kennedy was in complete control of the state party machinery!

News of the impressive victory spread throughout the country. Some Democratic leaders began to suggest Kennedy as a vice-presidential possibility. In the beginning he shrugged off the notion with a laugh. He was sure that as a Roman Catholic, he did not stand a chance. Politicians still remembered Alfred E. Smith, a Roman Catholic Governor of New York, who in 1928 had run as Democratic candidate for President against Republican Herbert Hoover and had been defeated.

Sorensen, however, disagreed with Kennedy. He was convinced the country had changed in the last thirty years. Moreover, he felt that even if his boss made a bid for the vice-presidential nomination and lost, it would help project him as a national figure for the future.

There was at least one factor in their favor, Sorensen argued. *Profiles in Courage* was scheduled for official publication in a matter of weeks, and advance sales indicated that it might be a best seller! This would help a great deal to boost the Kennedy chances. Still unconvinced, but fascinated by the challenge presented, Kennedy informed Sorenson that if he wished he was free to go ahead and solicit reaction to the prospect of his candidacy.

As Sorensen had guessed, *Profiles in Courage* was an immediate best seller. Foreign publishers placed bids to buy translation rights for a dozen different languages. Harper took out huge advertisements, and parts of the book were reprinted in newspapers and mass circulation magazines. Overnight, Kennedy found himself projected into the national spotlight as never before.

For Sorensen it was a green light. Some quiet political pulse-taking confirmed his own feeling that many politicians were not dead set against a Catholic candidate. He also discovered that Kennedy's political attractiveness was a salable commodity—he was young, handsome and well known. A "low-pressure" campaign was organized. Friendly governors, Congressmen and party leaders were quietly approached by Sorensen and other Kennedy aides and urged to talk with their friends about the young Senator from Massachusetts.

133

Sorensen even prepared a list of fifty people closest to Adlai Stevenson and sent them literature favorable to Kennedy—on the assumption that Stevenson would be the presidential candidate.

Kennedy himself wisely stayed out of the political maneuvering, but he kept abreast of developments. The main problem was the "Catholic issue"—the need to prove to politicians that Kennedy's religion would not hurt him at the polls. Here Sorensen played a trump card. He prepared a detailed analysis, using voting figures from the previous presidential election, to show that a Catholic on the ticket could *help* a Protestant candidate like Stevenson. He argued that since Eisenhower had made serious inroads in the large cities in 1952, it was important for the Democrats to win these urban areas back. Since Catholics were concentrated in the cities, a Catholic running mate not only would not hurt, but might make the difference between triumph and defeat!

It was a bold argument, skillfully presented. Sorensen quietly released the study to several leading magazines and newspapers. It created a bombshell. For the first time, objections to having a Catholic candidate had been met by an effective argument *in favor* of having a Catholic on the presidential ticket.

So successful was the study that Sorensen began to worry lest Kennedy grow too optimistic. They had agreed that if the campaign failed, neither was to be disappointed. When Sorensen sensed that his boss's hopes were rising, he warned bluntly, "I hope you're not going beyond our understanding."

Kennedy smiled wistfully. "Well, I must admit—I *will* be disappointed if I don't make it—at least for a few hours."

In truth, things were going so well that he had every reason to feel confident. Physically, he was almost free of pain; sales of the book were still soaring; and to his delight, Jackie was going to have a baby in the fall!

A hot wind from the west enveloped Chicago like an oppressive blanket when Senator and Mrs. Kennedy arrived in Chicago in the middle of August to attend the 1956 Democratic National Convention at the International Amphitheater. By the time their plane had landed, Jackie was feeling ill because of the heat and her pregnancy. It was agreed that she would stay at the home of Eunice and Sargent Shriver, for she and her husband knew that they would see little of each other during the convention.

Even before the convention opened, the Kennedy camp stepped up the pace of its campaign. In addition to his aides, the entire Kennedy clan was present, and everyone went to work meeting delegates and addressing delegations at breakfast and luncheon sessions. Sargent Shriver managed to buttonhole Adlai Stevenson for a few minutes to sell him on the virtue of Senator Kennedy as a vice-presidential running mate, since Stevenson's nomination was a foregone conclusion.

Traditionally it is the prerogative of the presidential nominee himself to choose the other half of the ticket, but Shriver shrewdly deduced from Stevenson's attitude that he might be willing to break precedent and allow the convention itself to make the choice. Shriver raced back to Kennedy with the news. Sorensen and the others felt that it was encouraging enough to warrant having the would-be candidate himself leave the wings and come out on the stage. Kennedy agreed.

He invited the entire New England delegation to a breakfast and let it be known informally, but with surprising frankness, that he would not be averse to running on Stevenson's ticket. Everybody present rose and pledged him solid support! Kennedy flushed with pleasure. "I should invite you all to breakfast every morning," he said with a grin.

Events continued to take a favorable turn. On the second night of the convention, he got an unexpected call from Adlai Stevenson. Would he agree to make the nominating speech on behalf of Stevenson the next day? Kennedy said yes immediately. But he couldn't help asking himself what it meant. Was Stevenson favorably inclined toward him? Or was the invitation an empty honor—a "consolation prize" signifying that Stevenson did not want him on the ticket?

Finally, he decided that it didn't matter, that the thing to do was simply to give the best speech of which he was capable. Accordingly, he and Sorensen labored all night on the text before they were satisfied. Then Kennedy grabbed a few hours of sleep, shaved, changed his clothes and went over to the convention hall. Virtually every paragraph of the speech brought tumultuous cheers. . . .

"We are here today selecting a man who must be more than something of a good candidate, more than a good politician, or a good liberal, or a good conservative," he declared. "We are selecting the head of the most powerful nation on earth—the man who literally will hold in his hands the power of survival or destruction, of freedom or slavery. . . .

"The grand alliance of the West, that chain for freedom . . . is cracking, and its unity deteriorating and its strength dissipating. . . ."

Adlai Stevenson won the nomination on the first ballot.

Kennedy decided that the time had come to make his play. Rivals were making bold bids for the vice-presidential spot: Averell Harriman and Mayor Robert Wagner of New York, Senator Estes Kefauver of Tennessee and others. The longer the delay, the more chance for other hopefuls to get into the act.

Following the lead of Sargent Shriver's earlier report, Kennedy instructed his aides to urge their friends in the Stevenson camp to try to persuade Stevenson to let the convention itself choose the vice-presidential candidate. The stratagem worked. Stevenson announced at once that he intended to depart from custom and put the choice up to the delegates.

For the Kennedy backers it was an important triumph, but there was no time for self-congratulations. The last-minute rush to line up delegates was on. Bobby Kennedy, Sargent Shriver, Kenneth O'Donnell, Larry O'Brien and the others rushed about trying to get groups of delegates before the opposition could do so.

On the morning of the third day of the convention the vice-presidential balloting began. Kennedy himself watched the proceedings on television from a room in the Stock Yard Inn, next door to the convention hall. With him were Ted Sorensen and some of the others who had no assignments on the convention floor.

The first ballot showed a number of "favorite son" nominations. Kennedy knew this was a normal development, but he couldn't help wondering who would inherit their votes on the second or third or fourth ballot. The vote tally on the first ballot showed Kefauver 483½, Kennedy 304, Gore 178, Wagner 162½, Humphrey 134½.

Now, as the second ballot got underway, the switching began. Kennedy forged ahead, winding up with 618 votes to Kefauver's 551½. He needed only 68 more votes for the nomination. At this point, somebody in the room congratulated him on a sure victory. But Kennedy said, "No, not yet."

The switching continued as the third ballot began, and now Kennedy found himself only 38 votes away. Suddenly, the Tennessee delegation announced a switch from Gore to Kefauver. Someone in the room moaned. Missouri followed by dropping Humphrey and transferring its votes to Kefauver. The stampede was on.

In a few minutes it was all over. Kefauver was the Democratic vice-presidential candidate!

As Kennedy entered the convention hall and marched up to the microphone to ask that Kefauver's nomination be made unanimous by acclamation, he appeared smiling and relaxed. But underneath there was tension, self-recrimination and pain.

Losing was not easy for any of the Kennedys. "Second best is a loser," his father used to say. He knew now what the admonition meant, more clearly than at any previous time in his life. He racked his brain to see if he had made any mistakes, and he turned his anger on himself for not having tried just a little bit harder.

Kennedy's nerves were brittle from the hectic convention. He was convinced that if he did not get away to unwind he would surely snap like an overtight spring. Yet Mrs. Kennedy, who was feeling worse than when they had arrived in Chicago, was in no mental or physical condition to travel. So it was agreed that he would fly to the Riviera for a short rest at his father's villa while she stayed at her stepfather's home in Newport.

A few days later Kennedy was relaxing aboard a sailboat on the gloriously blue Mediterranean. When he made port, an ominous cablegram was waiting for him. His wife was in the hospital after having undergone her second miscarriage, the message read, and the doctors were uncertain about her chances for survival.

He flew back to the United States immediately and took up a vigil at her bedside in Newport Hospital. With her life hanging in the balance, he prayed constantly for help. Finally the doctors held a consultation and, to his great relief, they announced that Mrs. Kennedy would be all right.

After Jackie's convalescence, Senator Kennedy leaped back into the political arena with zest. Although he had lost out on the nomination, he nevertheless campaigned with all his might for the Adlai Stevenson–Estes Kefauver ticket against the Republican slate of President Dwight D. Eisenhower and Richard M. Nixon. It was a hard-fought campaign which the Democrats lost. Kennedy could not help thinking that things had a habit of working out for the best, for if he had won the nomination the loss might very well have been blamed on the fact that a Roman Catholic was on the ticket.

Following the election, the Kennedys settled down to enjoy a more sedate existence. They had had little family life that year because of the convention and the election campaign, and Senator Kennedy felt a vague sense of guilt about it.

Mrs. Kennedy's ordeal in the hospital had brought them closer than ever before. Now that their marriage, which had started off on stormy seas, had reached tranquil waters, they discovered a new respect for each other as individuals and undertook to share each other's interests. Kennedy learned to enjoy French cooking which Jackie loved, and he began to visit art galleries and develop an interest in classical music. Under her prodding, he even became conscious of the importance of dressing neatly and smartly!

At the same time, Mrs. Kennedy enrolled in courses in history and political science at Georgetown University in order to be in a position to understand the things her husband cared about and to share them. These were subjects she had never liked, but she discovered that once she comprehended the nature of politics it could be terribly exciting. She also took up sports like water skiing and golf which Kennedy enjoyed but which she had never tried before.

Early in 1957, newspaper headlines announced that *Profiles in Courage* had been awarded the Pulitzer Prize in biography! The entire Kennedy clan was proud and delighted. Kennedy himself was personally pleased, and he and Ted Sorensen could not help but realize in addition how much it would boost his political stock.

To add to his good fortune, Mrs. Kennedy informed him that she was pregnant again. Because of her previous difficulty, she was plagued by a fear of losing this baby, too, but the Senator tried to reassure her.

On the day after Thanksgiving Day, 1957, she gave birth to a girl. The doctor reported that mother and baby were both doing well. They named the baby Caroline.

As the 1958 election approached, Kennedy began to prepare for his re-election campaign, since his first six-year term as a Senator was expiring. His record was respectable if not impressive. As a first-term Senator he had drawn a few committee memberships, but the only one that could be considered at all important was a seat on the Labor and Public Welfare Committee. His lack of seniority made it difficult to sponsor important national legislation.

As a result, most of the Kennedy-introduced bills were concerned purely with local Massachusetts problems, such as legislation to spur the state's economic growth by assisting her fishing and textile industries. Like most Senators, he obtained backing for these local bills by spending a good deal of time in the Senate cloakroom bartering support and convincing other legislators of the importance of his measures. He found that by adopting a sober, analytical approach he could win more votes than by threats or emotional appeals. Consequently, he gained a reputation among his colleagues as a cool, somewhat detached legislator, but at the same time he earned their deep respect for intellectual strength.

Kennedy's success in winning passage of legislation favorable to his home state raised his political stock enormously with the voters back home. However, in national affairs, too, he was beginning to establish a reputation, partly due to his role in the 1956 convention when he had emerged as a national figure, and partly as a result of his own growing political maturity.

On issues about which he felt strongly he gave unstinting support, often disregarding possible political consequences. For example, having developed into a staunch internationalist, he gave strong backing to legislation calling for additional foreign aid expenditures, even though his view was not shared by many of

141

his constituents. He also supported the role of the United Nations as a vehicle for settling international disputes, in spite of the fact that letters from a sizable number of Massachusetts voters, particularly in Boston, reflected isolationist sentiments.

On domestic matters, too, he took strong liberal positions. Since 1954, when the Supreme Court in its historic ruling had outlawed school segregation, no national issue had so gripped the attention of the American people as that of civil rights. From his vantage point in the Senate Kennedy realized that a new revolution was in the making. He became a strong advocate of federal action to guarantee equal rights for Negroes, even though many members of his own party from the South bitterly opposed such a policy and threatened to split the Democratic party. Late in 1957 he had flown down to Jackson, Mississippi—a segregationist stronghold—to address a group of southerners. The Republican state chairman of Mississippi, hoping to embarrass him and the Democratic party, challenged him to publicly declare himself on school desegregation.

With full recognition of the fact that it was an emotion-laden issue, Kennedy told the crowd forthrightly: "I have no hesitancy in telling the Republican chairman the same thing I said in my own city of Boston—that I accept the Supreme Court decision as the law of the land. I know that we do not all agree on that issue, but I think most of us do agree on the necessity to uphold law and order in every part of the land."

It was thus a solid if sometimes controversial record that Kennedy presented to the voters of Massachusetts as he prepared to run for re-election to the Senate in the fall of 1958. Yet even before the senatorial race got underway, he was already looking beyond the horizon to 1960. In two more years, he told himself, he would be ready to run for the Presidency of the United States.

11

REACHING FOR THE PEAK

The senatorial race of 1958 established Kennedy as a leading contender for the nation's top office. His personal popularity in Massachusetts reached tidal wave proportions. For the first time Mrs. Kennedy took an active part in a political campaign. She was at his side during most of his appearances and cooperated in the shooting of a TV film which emphasized their family life. It proved to be one of the most effective weapons in the entire campaign.

Kennedy was determined to stump every last corner of the state. An easy victory was a foregone conclusion, since his opponent, Vincent Celeste, was one of the weakest candidates the Republicans could have put up. But he wanted to win by a huge margin, hopeful that it would help his presidential aspirations.

His strategy proved sound. When the returns were in, he found he had polled 874,608 *more* votes than his opponent! It was the largest margin of victory ever recorded for any candidate for any office in the state. The performance was so astounding that Kennedy was immediately spotlighted as a front-runner for the Democratic presidential nomination in 1960.

He was keenly aware that there was a strong under-current of opposition to his nomination. Many politicians and citizens felt that he was merely a rich man's son out to buy the nomination. He couldn't help asking himself with a trace of bitterness whether his qualifications for political office would have been improved had he been a poor man forced to barter political favors for campaign funds.

Another barrier to his candidacy was his religion. He surmised that there were still pockets of intolerance throughout the country—places where voters would blindly cast their ballots *against* a Roman Catholic, any Roman Catholic. Yet he could not help agreeing with Ted Sorensen that the religious issue was no longer as important as if had been during the Al Smith campaign of 1928, for people had grown more tolerant. The nagging question was whether the delegates to a national convention could be won over to this point of view. True, at the 1956 convention he himself had come close to receiving the vice-presidential nomination in spite of his religion, but it was quite another matter to persuade a convention of hard-headed politicians that a Roman Catholic should head the ticket.

Sometimes, when playing happily with little Caroline on the beach at Hyannis Port during the summer of 1959, Kennedy could not resist analyzing his own motives in seeking the Presidency. Certainly the office itself was terribly demanding—it robbed a man of his years, very probably of his health and most definitely it constituted a burden on his family. Indeed, the Ambassador, who should know, had once pointed out from this standpoint being President of the United States was "the worst job in the world."

Why, therefore, would anyone want to become

President? Senator Kennedy asked himself. Was it ambition? Vanity? In his case was he simply trying to prove that a Roman Catholic could get himself elected to the highest office in the land? He was honest enough to admit that these considerations were a part of it. But there was something more. A vision of America perhaps, and the way America ought to be—and a desire on his part to play a role in realizing that vision.

When he and his brothers and sisters were young the Ambassador had never permitted them to forget that they had deep obligations to the country that had nurtured them and provided so bountifully for them. "Public service is the noblest profession I know of," Mr. Kennedy would tell them. He himself had underscored that precept by his own example. In recalling it now, Senator Kennedy knew instinctively that his own aspirations to become President of the United States were somehow rooted in the lessons learned in those half-forgotten days of his boyhood.

He sincerely believed that the nation was desperately in need of new and more vigorous leadership. Like other Democrats, he felt that President Dwight Eisenhower, though personally likable, had done little during his eight years in the White House to solve the nation's growing problems. His administration, Kennedy felt, had been one of bland inactivity. No great mistakes had been made, but neither had there been great accomplishment. While some argued that the philosophy of the Eisenhower years reflected the bland mood of the American people during the 1950's, Kennedy was convinced that this was not an acceptable explanation. The world had not stood still in those eight years, he told himself, and the job of national leadership was to awaken the people to that fact. But this the Eisenhower administration seemed incapable of doing.

The Communist world and the democracies were still locked in the vise of a cold war, and the threat of atomic annihilation was greater than ever as both sides had built up vast storehouses of missiles and nuclear warheads. In Asia and Africa, new nations representing over a billion people had thrown off the shackles of colonialism and were expressing their determination to be free. Other nations, cursed by the twin scourges of poverty and illiteracy, were threatening to undermine the political stability of vast areas of the world by serving as seedbeds of revolution and antidemocratic activity.

Facing the people of the United States, too, were urgent domestic problems that were waiting to be solved. The civil rights revolution, reflected in the pressing demands of the Negro people for guarantees of equality that had been denied them for almost a century, was being felt in every corner of the land. In many states, large scale pockets of poverty and unemployment had developed, intensifying the need for emergency action that would spur economic growth and provide relief from privation. And in fields like education and scientific progress, authorities were expressing grave fears that America was falling far behind in her ability to meet the legitimate needs of her people.

As Kennedy saw it, these were problems that could not be solved without active, vigorous national leadership. And more immediately, he was convinced of the need to alert the country to its problems, so the people could be awakened to their duties. Once the dormant energy of the United States was revived, the nation would begin to move ahead to a purposeful future, he felt.

In the late fall of 1959 the campaign to win the Democratic presidential nomination for Senator John F. Kennedy got under way. Although the entire Kennedy clan as well as a host of friends and aides were involved in the undertaking, it was Kennedy himself who devised the basic strategy and directed the entire operation.

In addition to the "Old Guard" like Sorensen, O'Donnell and O'Brien, who had been with him since the early days, there were some new faces: Pierre Salinger, a newspaperman and magazine writer from California who was to handle press relations; Louis Harris, an expert public opinion analyst; Stephen Smith, the husband of Kennedy's youngest sister, Jean, and the scion of a wealthy New York shipping family.

Kennedy's strategy was simple and direct. To win the nomination he knew he needed the support of grass roots Democrats throughout the country. To this end, a national "Kennedy Organization" would be established along the lines of his Massachusetts organization. Since his appeal in the past had proved to be most effective among young people and intellectuals, he would concentrate on these groups, making a special effort to reach teachers, college professors, writers and young business executives, for they were frequently important molders of public opinion in their areas. What's more, he would campaign vigorously in every corner of the land and appear before as many groups as possible, for he was convinced that by giving people a chance to see him and hear him in person he could help dispel the handicap of the religious issue that was sure to dog him.

Once he won the nomination, he would carry on an equally vigorous campaign against the Republican nominee. If the Republican standard bearer turned out to be Vice-President Richard Nixon, as the experts were predicting, then his campaign would be directed against the failures of the Eisenhower administration, in which Nixon was a key figure. On the positive side, he would call for new and vigorous leadership in Washington, pinpointing the crucial foreign and domestic problems which remained to be resolved. True, it would be an uphill fight all the way, but he was convinced that with effort and determination it was possible to achieve victory.

Soon the Kennedy campaign began to take shape with the opening of campaign offices in almost every state of the Union. Committees of prominent local civic leaders were organized. In some instances he secured the support of local politicians by offering to send in experts like public opinion analyst Harris or publicity man Salinger to help them with their local campaign problems.

One important decision Kennedy faced concerned participation in the presidential preference primaries. In the sixteen states in which these preconvention contests were held, the primaries served as an indicator of public opinion. They gave the people a chance to voice their sentiments as to their party's choice of a presidential candidate. While winning a primary might help a man's candidacy, losing it hurt his chances considerably. And in order to win, a grueling and expensive statewide campaign was usually required.

Many politicians hated the primaries, for they were convinced that they served no useful purpose. Some of Kennedy's advisers shared this sentiment and urged him not to risk his chances in primary fights, but he himself was convinced that if he could not show grass roots strength in the primaries, he could never win the support of the delegates at the national convention. Therefore, to the dismay of some of his aides, he announced he would enter seven of the sixteen primaries. The first important primary, in Wisconsin, would pit him against Senator Hubert Humphrey of Minnesota.

The winter's snow still blanketed much of the Midwest when Mr. and Mrs. Kennedy flew up to Wisconsin in March to launch the campaign.. The country seemed desolate as they traveled from town to town by motorcade, shaking hands and addressing street corner gatherings in an attempt to melt the icy hostility which many midwesterners showed toward the young Senator from the East. Mrs. Kennedy was faithfully on hand to add a touch of beauty and grace to the campaign party.

One day Kennedy was called back to Washington to vote on an important bill. In the interim, Mrs. Kennedy took over the job of campaigning. She had never made a political speech before, but she was an immediate success. Normally shy and retiring, she spoke simply and to the point. "We've been working so hard in Wisconsin," she told one group, "and I know that if you do see fit to support my husband you will find that you haven't misplaced your trust." In another town she said, "He has served his country fourteen years in the Navy and in Congress. He cares deeply about the welfare of his country, and as President could make the greatest contribution to its future."

When the primary election was held on April 5, Kennedy found that his efforts had not been in vain. The final tally showed a margin of victory of 106,000 votes over Senator Humphrey. It was a resounding triumph, one that echoed throughout the country. As a result, the public opinion polls now showed him to be the leading Democratic contender!

The political pundits, however, pointed out that the decisive test would come in West Virginia, a heavily Protestant state where it was believed the religious issue would be of great importance. Early polls had shown West Virginians seventy to thirty for Kennedy over Hubert Humphrey, but as the May 10 Primary Day approached, sentiment switched sharply. Public opinion expert Louis Harris reported that the voters now were sixty to forty in favor of Humphrey. The explanation? Many West Virginians had not known that Senator Kennedy was a Roman Catholic, and now that they knew, their opinions had changed.

For Kennedy the switch in voter sentiment was a disastrous development. Most of the top Kennedy aides were rushed down to West Virginia in a furious effort to "beef up" the campaign. Virtually the entire Kennedy family as well as his Choate, Harvard and Navy friends poured into the state to lend their support.

But Kennedy was soon convinced that he could not win unless the basic issue of his religion was resolved. As yet, the question of religious bias had not been discussed openly in the campaign, either by him or by Hubert Humphrey. Now he had to make a fundamental decision. Should he continue to back away from the issue? Or should he take the bull by the horns and discuss the matter frankly? It was a choice no one, not even Ted Sorensen, could make for him.

On April 25, Kennedy made what up to that time was probably the most important political decision of his life. He decided to attack the religious issue head-on and try to talk sense to the people of West Virginia and of the United States!

He knew that the principal opposition of many non-Catholics stemmed from a fear that a Roman Catholic owed his primary allegiance to his church, rather than to his country. This charge had been used by bigots for years to stir up anti-Roman Catholic sentiment.

For the next ten days Kennedy pounded away at the religious theme in his speeches. He hoped that by removing the subject from the dark shadows of rumor and exposing it to the light of frank discussion it would wither away as a basic issue. "I refuse to believe that I was denied the right to be President on the day I was baptized," he told the people of West Virginia.

On a TV show, he declared, ". . . when any man stands on the steps of the Capitol and takes the oath of office of President, he is swearing to support the separation of church and state; he puts one hand on the Bible and raises the other hand to God as he takes the oath. And if he breaks his oath, he is not only committing a crime against the Constitution for which the Congress can impeach him—and should impeach him —but he is committing a sin against God."

At this point Kennedy raised his hand as if from a Bible and repeated softly, "A sin against God, for he has sworn on the Bible."

In addition to the religious theme, he hammered away at the issue of poverty. The people of West Virginia were not strangers to economic privation. Ever since the decline of the coal industry, unemployment and suffering had been widespread. Kennedy, born and raised in luxury, stared for the first time in his life at the grim face of poverty and was shocked by its ugliness. He visited families living in shanties, whose subsistence consisted solely of government relief rations. He talked to little children whose legs were spindly from lack of a decent diet, and later he observed thoughtfully to an aide, "Imagine, just imagine kids who never drink milk!" He could not help wondering how, in the face of such hardship, people were able to retain their self-respect at all.

The exposure to the poverty of the mining fields was an emotional experience that had a profound effect on Kennedy. It sparked a sense of personal indignation that communicated itself in his speeches. There was a new fervor and sense of commitment in his attitude. If he were elected President, he vowed to himself, one of his first tasks would be to help the poor of West Virginia and their counterparts all over the country.

May 10, Primary Day, was a drizzly, cloudy day. As the voters went to the polls, the drizzle turned to rain. In Kennedy headquarters, the mood matched the weather. Weariness and uncertainty became the order of the day.

By nine in the evening, the first returns began to trickle in, showing a majority for Kennedy. As the total grew it became obvious that it was a rout. Shortly after one o'clock in the morning, Hubert Humphrey conceded defeat. At that moment Kennedy knew that he would be the next Democratic candidate for President.

Early in July, the delegates began to gather in Los Angeles for the Democratic National Convention. Mrs. Kennedy was pregnant again, so it was agreed that the Senator should go to the convention without her, for they recalled only too vividly the tragic events following the Chicago convention four years before.

From the time Kennedy landed in Los Angeles, there was little question that he was the leading contender. The Wisconsin and West Virginia primary victories had paid off in delegate support. Bobby Kennedy, Kenny O'Donnell, Larry O'Brien and the others put their heads together and added up over 600 committed votes, only 160 short of what was needed for nomination.

Now the Kennedy supporters began to work on the delegates in earnest. With quasi-military precision—walkie-talkie radios were used for communciation!—they went from delegation to delegation, cajoling, arguing, reassuring. In the drive for delegate strength it was soon clear that his leading rival would be Senator Lyndon B. Johnson of Texas, the Senate Majority Leader.

The other leading candidates were Senator Stuart Symington of Missouri and Adlai Stevenson, who had been defeated twice by Dwight Eisenhower. Although the two-time candidate insisted he was not interested in running again, crowds of Stevenson backers packed the Convention Hall and organized tumultuous demonstrations in a desperate effort to get a draft going for their favorite.

The polling itself was almost an anticlimax. The final tally showed 806 votes for Kennedy; 409 for Senator Johnson; 86 for Senator Symington; 79½ for Stevenson. All the others combined received 140½ votes. Senator Kennedy had been chosen on the very first ballot!

Now the maneuvering got underway for the vice-presidential nomination. In the hours following Kennedy's victory, he received deputations of political leaders wishing to press the nominations of their favorites. His aides also suggested various possibilities. The two names mentioned most often were Senator Stuart Symington of Missouri and Senator Henry M. Jackson of Washington. Kennedy had to admit that both were good men and popular men and either would make a reasonably strong candidate.

But another design was taking shape in his mind, one so far-fetched that he couldn't help grinning to himself in anticipation of the astonishment it would evoke. The one name everyone seemed to shy away from was that of Senator Lyndon B. Johnson, the runner-up in the presidential balloting. In the last-minute contest for delegate support between Johnson and himself, harsh feelings had been unleashed between the two camps, so the choice of Johnson was the last thing anyone would propose or expect.

But why not Johnson? Kennedy asked himself. Aside from the convention fight he had always been friendly with the Texan, for he was a man to be admired and respected. Politically, he would be an asset to the ticket, for he could help win the support of the South which was notoriously suspicious of rich young millionaires from Boston with a Harvard accent.

Johnson himself had been a poor boy who had gotten his start in Congress under President Franklin D. Roosevelt whom he had supported and admired. As a liberal southerner, his political philosophy was close to that of Kennedy himself, an important factor in running a campaign that would be consistent with the Democratic party's liberal platform.

Of course there was the question of whether Johnson would accept a vice-presidential bid. Several years earlier, he had suffered a heart attack. And while he had made a remarkable recovery, so that his condition now was as sound as ever, would he want to undertake the severe strain of a presidential campaign in return for second place on the ticket? Moreover, would his disappointment at being defeated for the presidential nomination cause him to reject the offer out of hand?

Kennedy knew that when all was said and done he, and he alone, would have to make the final decision as to whether or not to ask Johnson. A favorable sign was a telegram of congratulations which the Texan had sent him just after his victory. The tone was so warm and sincere, he sensed that Johnson did not harbor any permanent ill feelings. Nevertheless, he spent a long night and day weighing the pros and cons. He casually sounded out his aides and the political leaders who came to visit him in his suite on the desirability of having Johnson on the ticket.

The response was mixed. Some felt that the Senate Majority Leader was a perfect political choice. Others, particularly from the big cities, argued that while Johnson's record was excellent and they had nothing against him personally, they felt that voters would *think* of him as a conservative southerner because he came from Texas. As a result, they claimed, the ticket would be hurt in the big northern cities, particularly among labor and the minority groups.

After considering the various arguments, Kennedy could not help but feel that nothing he had heard so far was impressive enough to change his initial predisposition in favor of the Senate Majority Leader. The important thing was that Johnson's political record was eminently sound and he would be able to martial political support in the South, where it was desperately needed.

Earlier, some of Kennedy's aides had contacted some of Johnson's advisers to sound them out on the Texan's possible reaction to a vice-presidential bid, but there had been nothing specific, no definite offers or promises. Now, the presidential nominee decided not to wait any longer. He called Johnson's hotel suite directly and got him out of bed. Would Johnson be willing to accept the second place spot? he wanted to know.

The Senate Majority Leader, still sleepy, replied by asking if this meant the nomination were being offered to him. Kennedy read a draft of a statement which he himself had prepared, announcing the selection of Lyndon Baines Johnson as the vice-presidential candidate.

Johnson paused. What he wanted to know, he declared in his soft drawl, was whether Kennedy *really* wanted him or not. The presidential nominee answered directly and without hesitation. Yes, he did want him and felt the ticket needed him.

In that case, Senator Johnson told him, he would accept the offer to serve on the ticket.

It was a tired but inspired presidential nominee who stepped up to the microphone on the last day of the convention to formally accept the mantle of candidacy. Seated on the platform were his mother and sisters and all the men he had defeated—Humphrey, Symington, Johnson and Stevenson. Kennedy spoke eloquently, from a text on which he and Sorensen had labored hard the night before.

". . . The times are too grave, the challenge too urgent, the stakes too high to permit the customary passions of political debate," he declared. "We are not here to curse the darkness, but to light the candle that can guide us through that darkness to a safe and sane future. . . .

". . . The problems are not all solved and the battles are not all won—and we stand today on the edge of a New Frontier—the frontier of the 1960's—a frontier of unknown opportunities and perils—a frontier of unfulfilled hopes and threats. . . ."

Kennedy paused, breathed deeply and concluded:

"It has been a long road . . . to this crowded convention city. Now begins another long journey, taking me into your cities and homes all over America. Give me your help. . . ."

The crowd cheered.

"Give me your hand—" the roar became ear-deafening "—your voice and your vote."

The thousands of delegates and spectators who had jammed the convention hall were on their feet now, cheering and applauding and shouting words of encouragement and support.

A new champion had accepted the call of the party of Thomas Jefferson, Andrew Jackson, Woodrow Wilson and Franklin Delano Roosevelt.

Two weeks later the Republican party held its convention in Chicago. The results surprised no one, for like the Democratic convention the outcome had been almost unanimously predicted. Richard Nixon, Vice-President under Dwight Eisenhower, was selected overwhelmingly on the first ballot. As his running mate he chose Henry Cabot Lodge, United States delegate to the United Nations.

From the very first, Kennedy waged his campaign against Nixon with his usual skill and efficiency. Faced with the religious issue, he brought it out in the open as he had done in West Virginia. Crisscrossing the country by plane, he visited 237 cities, speaking, shaking hands, answering reporters' questions.

Kennedy's basic strategy was simple enough: attack the Eisenhower Administration, which Nixon represented, for doing too little to solve the nation's crucial foreign and domestic problems while at the same time communicating a picture of Kennedy youth, vigor and determination. In his acceptance speech in Los Angeles, he had spoken of a "New Frontier" of opportunity and peril—and he proceeded to reiterate this theme in speech after speech. He spoke impassionedly of the necessity for new effort and vigor—he pronounced it *vigah*—in searching for ways to reduce cold war tension; of the importance of combating still-existing poverty in the United States as well as abroad; of the critical need to extend equal rights to Negroes who had been denied them for a hundred years. And always he emphasized that he was offering the people, not solutions, but challenges. "My call is to the young in heart, regardless of age," he told his audiences.

It was a remarkable and daring departure from conventional campaign themes. Instead of offering a platform of glib promises, he was asking for greater citizen responsibility and individual sacrifice. Many political experts opined that it was hardly the way to win over an electorate which, they claimed, was constantly searching for a "father image" to assume the burden of all national decisions. To this argument, Kennedy calmly replied that he was convinced the American voter was mature enough to accept the unvarnished facts of national life, and he continued to pursue this theme to the despair of some of the old-time Democratic campaign strategists.

Another question he had to resolve was where to concentrate his personal efforts as the campaign grew hotter. In the early days, he had managed to cover hundreds of cities and 17,000 miles, but as the need for intensive campaigning increased, he realized there was just so much territory that he himself could visit with any degree of effectiveness.

Nine large states—New York, Pennsylvania, California, Michigan, Texas, Illinois, Ohio, New Jersey and Massachusetts—seemed to hold the key to the election. Together, they accounted for 237 of the 269 electoral votes needed to elect a president. Except for California and Texas, they were all in the Northeast and Middle West. If he could concentrate his major effort on the important industrial Northeast, Lyndon Johnson would take care of Texas. And Adlai Stevenson, who was popular in California and had promised to campaign vigorously for him, would take care of the West Coast. If he could make a clean sweep of the critical nine states, that left only sixty or seventy electoral votes needed for victory. He counted on Johnson picking up at least sixty in southern states other than Texas, and a few of the smaller New England and Midwestern states that normally went Democratic to provide a healthy margin of victory.

It seemed simple enough—on paper. But in actual practice it meant fatigue, endless speechmaking and rushing to and fro, always behind schedule. He lived on hot dogs, hamburgers, malteds and tomato soup, gulping his meals on the run and getting most of his sleep while sprawled in the seat of the family airplane "Mother Ship," later renamed the "Caroline." He was grateful, however, for one blessing—his back had not acted up in a long while and this fact in itself at least made campaign life bearable.

Kennedy did not pretend to be an orator. He wanted to talk sense to the American people, and he did so in a style that would have made some professors of elocution wince. Standing bareheaded, with his sandy hair tousled from the fall wind, he would point a finger at an outdoor audience shivering from the cold, and ram home his arguments like pistol shots, in his broad Harvard-Boston accent. Sometimes his voice would rise in pitch, straining his vocal cords, and at other times the words would tumble out too fast and he would begin to stutter. But it didn't faze him, for he believed content was more important than sonorous oratory. "These guys who can make the rafters ring with hokum—well, I guess that's okay, but it keeps me from being an effective political speaker," he explained to one curious reporter.

Early in September representatives of both candidates participated in an extraordinary meeting in New York City with executives of the nation's two largest broadcasting networks. It proved to be a fateful conference. The purpose was to discuss the possibility of a series of television debates in which Kennedy and Nixon would face each other on the same platform in full view of the American people! Such a confrontation of presidential candidates was unprecedented.

Some of Kennedy's advisers were not happy with the proposal. Nixon was reputed to be an expert debater. Furthermore, he had established himself as a master in the use of the television for political campaigning.

Yet in spite of these drawbacks, Kennedy saw important advantages in agreeing to the debates. As Vice-President for eight years, Nixon was familiar to everyone. Kennedy, on the other hand, was still the little-known challenger in many corners of the nation, despite his endless campaigning. Here, then, was an opportunity to win tremendous exposure without cost and allow the people to compare the merits of both candidates at point-blank range. And since one of

Nixon's favorite tactics was to accuse him of being too "immature" to be President—Kennedy at forty-three was only four years younger than Nixon—this would be a superb chance to disprove the charge.

After careful deliberation, Kennedy gave his approval to the debate plan. Nixon, who saw these talks as a good opportunity to knock off his rival with a single master blow, assented eagerly.

By the middle of September, everything had been arranged. There were to be four debates spaced approximately a week apart, with each of the three major networks alternating as producer. A panel of four representatives of the press would be on hand to ask questions. The candidates would deliver an opening and closing statement of eight minutes each in the first and last debate. The candidates would have two and a half minutes each to answer questions put to them by the press panel.

On Sunday, September 25, Kennedy arrived in Chicago where the first debate was to take place the following day. With him were Ted Sorensen and two other assistants, Richard Goodwin and Mike Feldman. They had brought with them a footlocker stuffed with reference materials.

Kennedy went about the task of preparing for the debate as if he were cramming for an exam. For twenty-four hours he busily absorbed facts and figures on every conceivable subject area. While he was confidentially familiar with all the possible issues that could be raised, he knew that a demonstrated mastery of the latest data was essential, for a single slip or uncertain hesitation would simply give weight to Nixon's charge that he was inexperienced and unfamiliar with governmental problems.

When Kennedy showed up at the Columbia Broadcasting studios in Chicago, the Vice-President was already there. Kennedy was wearing a dark gray suit, but he noticed that Nixon was wearing one of a much lighter shade, so that on the monitor, his adversary seemed to fade into the pale gray walls of the studio. A minor tactical advantage, he told himself, but an advantage all the same. In addition, the Vice-President seemed weary and tense.

Finally, all was ready. The moderator was Howard K. Smith, a well-known television news commentator. Smith made an opening announcement to the television and radio audience, and suddenly, they were on the air before seventy million Americans.

The initial statements went smoothly enough, but once the questioning began, Kennedy noticed a curious thing. Although he took pains to address himself to the people of the United States, Nixon seemed to ignore the unseen audience and concentrate on his adversary, as if he were participating in a college debating tournament and a group of judges were scoring them on points.

On each issue Kennedy cited facts and statistics with precision. In spite of the glare of the studio lights, he could see from the reaction of the press representatives that his mastery of detail was making an impact. Nixon, on the other hand, continued to tag along, trying to rebut his opponent's points without ever really taking the offensive.

At the end of the first debate, Kennedy's advisers congratulated him on a splendid showing. Louis Harris' public opinion samplings showed an astonishingly favorable reaction to Kennedy's performance. "Each time we're going to gain and he's going to lose," one of

Kennedy's aides observed with a grin about his appearances on the television screen with Nixon.

The prediction proved accurate. Each succeeding debate gave Kennedy an added opportunity to show his knowledge and his quick wit. After the final appearance on October 21, many political observers felt that while Nixon had been hurt somewhat, Kennedy had been helped enormously because of the tremendous exposure the programs had provided.

Now, with less than three weeks to go, both candidates campaigned harder than ever. One of the all-important question marks was how the civil rights revolution taking place would affect the election. Since the Supreme Court decision of 1954 outlawing school segregation, a new spirit of hope and militancy had been sparked in the American Negro. One of the most revered heroes of the Negro's struggle to achieve equality was a soft-spoken minister from Atlanta, Martin Luther King, Jr.

On October 19, Dr. King had been arrested with fifty-two other Negroes for refusing to leave a segregated restaurant in an Atlanta department store. The other "sit-ins" were released, but the civil rights leader was sentenced on a technicality to four months of hard labor! Soon there were rumors that he would be lynched—that the white officials had no intention of allowing him to leave the prison alive.

When word of Dr. King's plight reached the Kennedy campaign staff, an aide suggested to Kennedy's brother-in-law, Sargent Shriver, that the candidate himself telephone Mrs. King to assure her of his concern and his readiness to intervene to obtain her husband's release.

Kennedy's reaction to the idea was swift and spon-

taneous. Without bothering to weigh the possible political consequences—it was clear that the white South
would not react favorably to such a move—he immediately put through a long-distance call to Mrs. King,
comforting her and pledging support. At the same time,
Bobby Kennedy telephoned the Georgia judge who had
set the sentence and pleaded that Dr. King be released.

The following day the Negro leader, unharmed, was
released from jail on bail pending appeal.

Although no attempt had been made by the Kennedy organization to exploit the incident and it received scant notice in the press, Mrs. King told some of
her friends about it. Soon word echoed across the
nation's Negro communities like a clarion call. Typical
was the reaction of Martin Luther King, Sr., father of
the civil rights leader and himself a Baptist minister.
A few weeks before, he had come out for Richard
Nixon, but now he reversed his position. "Because
this man," he said of Kennedy, "was willing to wipe
the tears from my daughter [in-law]'s eyes, I've got a
suitcase of votes, and I'm going to take them to Mr.
Kennedy and I'm going to dump them in his lap."

Election Day dawned at last. Early on the morning
of November 8, Kennedy, accompanied by Mrs. Kennedy who was soon to give birth, drove to a polling
place in Boston's Third Precinct and voted. Then they
made the twenty-five-minute flight to Hyannis Port and
had breakfast with the Kennedy clan.

Later, the presidential candidate and his brothers
tossed a football back and forth. However, when the
Ambassador came out, his oldest son joined him on the
porch for a quiet father-to-son talk.

In the afternoon, Kennedy played with little Caroline, finally kissing her good night and sending her up-

stairs to bed. As the sun set, some early returns began to trickle in. Everyone now sat glued to the television sets, watching and waiting. At eleven o'clock Mrs. Kennedy retired, but the candidate remained downstairs with the others. It now appeared that the race would be a close one. Finally at three forty in the morning, with the outcome still unresolved, Kennedy ate a sandwich, said good night and went to bed.

At seven o'clock, a squad of Secret Service men quietly infiltrated the Kennedy compound and threw a cordon around the house. A little later, Ted Sorensen raced upstairs to inform Kennedy, who was still in his pajamas and seated sleepily on the edge of his bed, that he was now President of the United States.

The final count showed 303 electoral votes for Kennedy and 219 for Nixon. However, the popular vote totals were astonishingly close. Only 112,881 votes out of a grand total of almost 69,000,000 separated the two candidates—a margin of one tenth of one percent!

There was still another exciting event to cap a tumultuous year. On Thanksgiving Day Mrs. Kennedy was rushed to Georgetown Hospital in Washington. There she gave birth to a healthy baby boy. They named him John F. Kennedy, Jr.

Eight weeks later, on January 20, 1961, Kennedy was inaugurated as the thirty-fifth President of the United States of America.

12

MR. PRESIDENT

The inauguration of John F. Kennedy took place in a world that he himself would hardly have recognized just fifteen years earlier. In the decade and a half since World War II, new forces had swept the globe.

In Africa, great colonial empires had been broken up, and new nations were emerging, reflecting the eternal drive of men to be free. But in other areas of the world the opposite had taken place, and freedom was being trampled under the heel of Communist totalitarianism. In Eastern Europe, China and Cuba, dictatorship and repression rather than freedom seemed to be the wave of the future. Indeed, in Cuba, just ninety miles from the United States, Fidel Castro, a bearded zealot, had successfully overthrown a tyrannical government in order to substitute his own brand of tyranny in the name of communism and try to "export" it to other nations of Latin America where people were mired in poverty and despair.

Against this backdrop of international tension was the terrifying shadow of nuclear destruction. Ever since 1945, when a great mushroom cloud had risen over Hiroshima in Japan, signifying the world's first atom bombing, the fear of nuclear warfare had never been far from human consciousness. Only mutual fear, a realization by the leaders of Soviet communism and the democracies that atomic war would mean total destruction for all, had helped maintain a kind of temporary balance of terror.

Time and again during the decade of the 1950's, representatives of both sides had met to try to work out an agreement for the eventual control of nuclear weapons, but mutual distrust proved to be an effective barrier to the signing of such a treaty. The democracies, led by the United States, had refused to accept any nuclear agreement unless it provided for periodic inspections within a country's borders by an international body like the United Nations to guarantee against "cheating." The Soviet Union, on the other hand, argued that inspections were merely a scheme to enable the West to indulge in spying operations. The issue of inspections could be discussed *after* the signing of a treaty providing for total international disarmament, the spokesmen declared. And there the controversy continued to rest after more than a decade of negotiations during which the world hovered on the brink of nuclear disaster.

But for the United States, the issue of freedom was not restricted to international matters alone. On another level, it constituted a domestic challenge that went forth to the fundamental roots of democracy. Confronted by the spreading civil rights revolution within its borders, the nation at last found itself face to face with the need to resolve once and for all a century-old American dilemma—the question of the Negro's place in American society. Was he to continue to be denied the freedom guaranteed all citizens by the Constitution of the United States? Or was he at long last to be granted full rights to pursue the highest level of his aspirations as a human being based on individual ability alone?

Yet the issue of freedom takes many forms, and few are more basic than freedom from want and despair. And here, too, America was approaching a critical juncture in its development. At a time when the standard of living for the country as a whole was the highest in its history, some twenty percent of its citizens continued to live in conditions of poverty that seemed to defy human reason and logic. It was a paradox made even more complicated by the development of increasingly efficient "automated" machines which threatened to throw more and more people out of work by eliminating their jobs, thus relegating them to the scrap heap of unemployment and disillusionment.

These, then, were some of the forces at work as the world witnessed the inauguration of John F. Kennedy in January of 1961. They were the conditions of contemporary human existence which he had tried to describe in his Inaugural Address, conditions which he saw, not only as threats, but as historic challenges to be accepted by a free people committed to great ends.

In the weeks prior to his taking office he had given a great deal of thought to the men who would be officially responsible for the major areas of his administration. His personal aides, like Ted Sorensen, Kenny O'Donnell and Larry O'Brien, would remain with him, of course, as would Pierre Salinger, who accepted the post of press secretary. But in addition he was required to have an official cabinet to help him run the government. As Chief Executive he was accountable for nine major departments, 104 bureaus, 12 sections, 108 services, 51 branches, 631 divisions, 19 administrations, six agencies, four boards, six commands, 20 commissions, 19 corporations, 10 headquarters, three authorities and 263 miscellaneous organizations!

With the help of aides, friends, family and former colleagues in the legislature, he had screened hundreds of recommendations for cabinet appointment, and in the end he had come out with a curiously diverse group. They were diverse in age, temperament, political outlook and experience. In fact, the only two qualities which he insisted they have in common were ability and loyalty to him as President.

The new cabinet consisted of Luther H. Hodges, a white-haired, twinkly-eyed grandfather and former governor of North Carolina, as Secretary of Commerce; crew cut Stewart L. Udall, a former Congressman from Arizona, as Secretary of the Interior; Robert S. McNamara, a Republican, who had resigned as president of the Ford Motor Company to become Secretary of Defense; Dean Rusk, former president of the Rockefeller Foundation, as Secretary of State; C. Douglas Dillon, a leading stockbroker who had been President Eisenhower's Undersecretary of State for Economic Affairs, as Secretary of the Treasury; former Minnesota governor, Orville Freeman, as Secretary of Agriculture; J. Edward Day, an attorney from Illinois who had once been Adlai Stevenson's legislative aide, as Postmaster-General; Arthur Goldberg, who had served as counsel for the steelworkers' union, as Secretary of Labor; and former Connecticut governor, Abraham Ribicoff, as Secretary of Health, Education and Welfare. Two-time presidential aspirant Adlai Stevenson was appointed Ambassador to the United Nations.

Only in his choice of Attorney-General did the

President-elect have any trouble persuading a nominee to join the cabinet. The nominee was his own brother Robert! From the outset, he was convinced that Bobby was the right man for the job. The younger Kennedy had been a counsel for many legislative committees. As chief rackets investigator for a Senate committee investigating labor racketeering, he had uncovered evidence of murder, extortion and misuse of funds by criminals who had infiltrated some unions. Moreover, in the eight years since he had headed his brother's first senatorial campaign, he had become a master political strategist whose talents and counsel the new administration sorely needed.

Both brothers felt that if the appointment of Bobby as Attorney-General were to be announced, there would be loud protests and charges of nepotism. But after careful consideration, the President decided that fear of criticism should not be allowed to divert him from what he knew was the right decision. He asked his brother to join the cabinet.

Bobby agonized over the offer. He, even more than the President, was sensitive to the possibility that his appointment might hurt his brother's brand-new administration. So he finally telephoned to say that he had decided to turn down the job. But he of all people had not reckoned with the Kennedy determination. The President invited him to breakfast the next morning, and for more than an hour used his prerogative as older brother to cajole, plead and even demand that the younger Kennedy change his mind.

Robert Kennedy finally agreed to accept.

Curiously enough, the mass outcry of protest they both had feared never materialized. Except for some funny and not-so-funny jokes about the "Kennedy dynasty" that made the rounds in Washington and elsewhere, and some raised eyebrows among editorial writers for a few Republican newspapers, the American public did not rise up in arms or anger to chastise its new President.

In addition to his regular aides and cabinet, the President appointed a number of special assistants and advisers to his staff, many of them from university faculties. His own alma mater, Harvard, was so heavily represented by men like the distinguished historian, Arthur Schlesinger, Jr., that some political columnists warned in mock alarm that if the raid on the Harvard campus continued the institution would have to close its doors for lack of staff!

During his campaign for the Presidency, John F. Kennedy had spoken of the things that troubled him— that troubled America. He had asked the nation to journey with him to a *New Frontier* to wage a struggle against the common enemies of man: tyranny, poverty, disease and war itself. And he had meant it.

Now, he lost no time in putting some of his words into action. Recalling the abject poverty of West Virginia which he had seen, he made it one of his first orders of business to have Orville Freeman, the new Secretary of Agriculture, double the ration of surplus foods distributed by the federal government to the five million jobless and needy families in the United States.

At his inauguration, he had spoken of setting up an "alliance for progress" for Latin-American countries. As far back as their original settlement, many of the nations of the Western Hemisphere below the United States–Mexican border had suffered grievously from poverty, illiteracy and economic underdevelopment. The result had been political unrest reflected in pe-

riodic revolutions and resentment against the wealthy
Yankee colossus to the north.

Within a few weeks of taking office the President
announced that he was putting into motion a program
to accelerate Latin-American economic, social and
technical development. It would be known as the
Alliance for Progress and would take place over a ten-
year period at a cost of twenty billion dollars in foreign
aid. This alliance would be a cooperative program, he
declared. The Latin-American nations themselves
would be expected to establish effective planning machinery, mobilize their domestic resources and develop
well-conceived and technically sound projects. Thus
it would be a sharp departure from many existing
foreign aid programs in which funds were given out by
the United States reluctantly and accepted resentfully
by poorer countries as a form of "charity."

During his campaign, too, Kennedy had spoken
about creating a new kind of foreign aid project—a
Peace Corps—that would harness the idealism and
energies of the youth of America. Instead of food or
money, the program would provide underdeveloped
countries in Africa, Asia and Latin America with
trained manpower to help develop their educational
facilities, health services, agriculture and industry.

Actually, the idea had not originated with Kennedy.
It had been advanced half a century earlier by the
famous philosopher and psychologist William James.
James had suggested a youth peace army which would
use military methods to tackle necessary but unpleasant civilian projects. To Kennedy, the plan had enormous appeal. Not only would it provide a way of giving technical assistance to needy lands but it would be
a beacon for American youth, many of whom felt life

lacked challenge. Kennedy knew that it was the young people who, more than any other group, needed a sense of purpose and personal commitment if the nation were to get moving again. He was convinced that the bland, uninspiring decade of the 1950's had dulled the idealism of the new generation.

In addressing the youth of America, he said, "Our generation has been frustrated in wanting to participate in foreign affairs, but we have had no outlet. The Peace Corps gives us a chance to go out and solve the problems we hear so much about day by day."

It was a bold and challenging concept. Many experts criticized it as visionary and impractical, but Kennedy was not deterred. One of his first public acts was to announce that he was asking for an appropriation for the immediate organization of a Peace Corps. Congress granted $30,000,000 for the first year. The Peace Corps was to be set up as a semi-independent agency within the Department of State. In searching for a director for the new organization, the President decided on his brother-in-law, R. Sargent Shriver, Jr. A former head of the Chicago Board of Education who had long been active in social service and youth work, Shriver appeared to be the perfect choice.

The new director set to work immediately on the myriad details involved in establishing the Peace Corps. Membership would be open to United States citizens eighteen years of age or older. Each volunteer would agree to serve for two years. The salary was to be nominal—it would consist of a modest allowance for living costs and incidental expenses and a mustering-out bonus to be paid when the Corpsman returned to the United States.

All applicants were to take a demanding test to determine their knowledge of the United States, its government and history as well as their ability to learn. Volunteers would be chosen on the basis of test scores, personal references, maturity, special skills and performance during a rigid training period. After a period of exhaustive training, the Peace Corpsman would be sent to work in an underdeveloped country, on a project established at the request of the government of the country involved. The Corpsmen would serve as conservationists, teachers, engineers, hygienists, bridge-builders, road surveyors, or in one of a number of other capacities.

Although the experts were critical of the plan, the youth of America was not. The response was far beyond the President's wildest hopes, particularly from the college campuses. From every corner of the land thousands of applications began to pour into Washington. It seemed as though the young people had suddenly awakened from a dreamlike torpor and were now ready to assume a real role in society. Through the Peace Corps Kennedy had thus managed to convey his own sense of purpose to an entire generation. Taking note of the amazing response to his call to service, he pointed out that at last the young people of America had been given an opportunity "not to change the world, necessarily, but to make it a better place."

"The energy, the faith, the devotion which we bring to this endeavor," he declared, "will light our country and all who serve it—and the glow from that fire can truly light the world."

As the first ten weeks of the new President's term drew to a close he could reflect with satisfaction that the journey to the New Frontier had gotten off to a good start. Announcement of the Alliance for Progress and the Peace Corps were significant triumphs in the campaign to "get America moving again," and had been greeted as such by a good part of the nation. In fact, editorial reaction in newspapers across the country, as well as the mail that poured into the White House daily, made it clear that the American people had been watching the initial activity of the incoming Chief Executive closely and liked what they saw. Without question, things seemed to be going even better than expected for the fledgling administration—even many of the Republican newspapers had to admit that.

But on April 17, 1961—less than three months from the time John F. Kennedy had taken office—a disaster took place off the coast of Cuba that took the bloom off some of his earlier successes and deeply shook his confidence in his own ability to serve in the most important job in the world.

Cuba, which had been freed from Spain by the United States after the Spanish-American War of 1898, had gone through an agonizing period. For nearly thirty-five years its people had lived through a succession of military revolts by ambitious army officers and governments run by ruthless, ironfisted dictators. In 1952, a former army sergeant named Fulgencio Batista took over the government by a military coup and installed himself as head. A year later, a group of rebels, sickened by the corruption and cruelty in the government, began a campaign of guerrilla warfare under the leadership of Fidel Castro, a young lawyer who promised to institute democratic reforms as soon as Batista was deposed.

In January, 1959, after almost six years of warfare, Batista fled to exile and Castro established a new government with himself as premier. But to the amazement and dismay of many of his own followers, he soon revealed himself as a self-avowed Communist and proceeded to install a Soviet-style dictatorship, instead of the democracy he had promised. With the help of Russia and Communist China, he also established Cuba as a base in the Western Hemisphere for the dispatching of trained agitators, propaganda materials and military equipment to dissident groups in other Latin-American countries in an attempt to stimulate the spread of Communist revolutionary activity.

Throughout his presidential campaign, Kennedy had bitterly criticized the Eisenhower Administration for allegedly doing nothing about the Communist threat so close to American shores. Shortly after winning the election, however, the President-Elect received a briefing from Allen Dulles, head of the Central Intelligence Agency. To his surprise, he learned that the Eisenhower Administration *had* been planning to do something about Castro—an invasion of Cuba! Already, hundreds of Cuban refugees from Castro's tyranny were training in Florida, Texas and Guatemala for a military landing on Cuba. According to the plan, the invasion itself was to be the spark that was to touch off a revolution of anti-Castroites in Cuba itself. Those opposed to the Castro regime were reputed to number in the hundreds of thousands. Moreover, while the strategy called for the American government to train and equip the Cuban invaders, help them plan the action and advise them in any way possible, the United States would not at any time intervene directly with its own military forces.

The President-Elect's initial reaction had been one of grave doubt, if not shock. The morality of such an attack seemed open to question. Wouldn't the nation and the world consider it an act of aggression? True, United States forces would not actually participate in the fighting, but America would still have to bear responsibility as the promoter of the invasion.

Yet after reflection, he could not help thinking that toppling Castro would be a blow for freedom, a way of redeeming for the Cuban people the revolution that had been stolen from them and turned into a Communist coup by the bearded demagogue.

Having thus succeeded in partially resolving his own moral dilemma, Kennedy began to concern himself with the practicability of the plan immediately upon taking office. There were about fourteen hundred Cuban refugees who had been welded into a fairly skillful and courageous fighting force. Could such a small army effectively carry out an invasion? Were the Cubans on the island as ready to rise up against Castro as some seemed to believe?

He turned these questions over in his mind with more than just a twinge of skepticism. However, the more he questioned the professional military and intelligence officials, the more confident they seemed of the workability of their plan. Some of the nonexperts, like Senator William Fulbright of Arkansas and a few others who knew of the invasion scheme, questioned it on moral and military grounds, but in the end President Kennedy decided to stick with professional experts.

While adhering to the basic strategy devised under Eisenhower, he laid down certain prohibitions in an effort to strengthen the nation's moral position. Under no circumstances was there to be participation in the actual fighting by American troops. Even the air support, consisting of a flight of antiquated B-26 medium bombers, were to be manned by Cuban pilots. Further, the planes were to be limited to two "airstrikes" against Cuban airfields—the first, two days prior to the landing, the second, on the morning of the invasion itself. The purpose was to give the world the impression that the action was a small-scale "raid" rather than a full-fledged war featuring massive air action. Although the restriction on air support would hinder the Cuban rebels, the President had been assured by the CIA that once the battle was under way and hundreds of thousands on the island took up arms and joined the landing party, Castro's government would be smashed in a matter of hours or days anyway.

As the plan for the invasion went ahead at full speed, Kennedy found himself caught up more and more in the excitement of the action. Some of his earlier doubts seemed to disappear and he became increasingly fascinated by the daring and glamour of the plan.

The fateful week arrived. With two days remaining until the landing, the Cuban-manned B-26's took off on schedule and bombed the Cuban airfields in an attempt to wipe out Castro's air force. They succeeded in destroying about half a dozen planes on the ground, but since the Cuban army had fifty-five planes, the results could hardly be considered spectacular. Even worse, as soon as the news of the bombing raid was blazoned in news headlines throughout the world, editorial attacks both inside the United States and abroad grew steadily, for it was quite obvious that the air strike could not have taken place without the knowledge and assistance of the American government.

Worried over the unexpectedly heavy criticism, even in countries that were normally friendly to the United States, the President and his advisers decided to cancel the second air strike. The CIA protested sharply at this last-minute change of plan, but the Administration insisted that the decision would have to stand.

Early in the morning of April 17, landing craft containing the Cuban invasion force assembled off the Cuban coast at a place called the Bay of Pigs; there, according to plan, the ships began a run for the shore. Almost at once, they ran into trouble. Castro's coastal observers detected the hostile forces, and four jet fighters armed with rockets were immediately dispatched. Two of the invasion ships loaded with ammunition and communications equipment were sunk.

Back in Washington, the President received the news almost as soon as it happened. Each succeeding report seemed to indicate that the invasion was going from bad to worse. The Cuban refugees were fighting bravely, he learned, but the skimpiness of their numbers and the lack of air cover had hurt the effort. However, a truly disastrous factor was the failure of the Cuban people to revolt on signal *as the CIA had assumed they would*. Either the intelligence had been inaccurate, or communication with the rebels on the island had been poor, or the experts had substituted a healthy dose of wishful thinking for down-to-earth facts.

Whatever the reasons for the failure, the President was sick at heart. The communiqués left no doubt that the grandiose scheme was turning into a costly debacle. The invaders who were still alive were now short of food and ammunition. To make matters worse, they were being attacked by tanks.

Within seventy-two hours after the rebel force had assembled at the Bay of Pigs, the "invasion" was over.

Survivors of the tiny force had no alternative but to lay down their arms and march into Castro's prisons.

For Kennedy it was a bitter and humiliating defeat. Good men had died needlessly. America's prestige was suffering as newspapers and diplomatic observers throughout the world began to accuse the United States of aggression and ineptness.

In the pall of gloom that settled on the White House, the President could not help holding himself responsible. He should have looked more closely at the plan. How could everybody involved have thought it could possibly succeed? True, he had been badly misled by the experts; yet he himself should have asked more questions and evinced more doubts and listened more carefully to men like Senator Fulbright and some of the other nonexperts.

Ninety days had passed since he first took office. He had badly bungled the first major crisis facing his administration. Only his family and closest friends and aides, like brother Bobby, Ted Sorensen, Kenny O'Donnell and Larry O'Brien, could comprehend the real depth of his hurt. At one meeting, O'Donnell leaned over to Pierre Salinger and muttered, "That's the first time Jack Kennedy ever lost anything."

As the weeks passed, the President was better able to re-examine the affair soberly. He saw that the mistake of the Bay of Pigs fiasco could at least provide guidance for the future. For one thing, it had taught him that the weeds of Castro influence in the Western Hemisphere would have to be isolated and choked out gradually, not removed forcibly. He had also come to the realization that something was dreadfully wrong with the intelligence structure of the country, so he ordered a complete investigation of the CIA.

His father told him that Cuba was the best lesson he could have had early in his administration. The President could not entirely accept the Ambassador's optimistic view, for the United States and the Cuban invaders had paid dearly for the error. Nevertheless, he agreed that since it *had* happened, it would be doubly tragic if he were to learn nothing from the experience.

The President rejected any suggestion that he disclaim personal responsibility for the affair. He had made the final decision, and he personally would accept the blame. On April 18 he addressed a meeting of the American Society of Newspaper Editors. The speech was televised throughout the nation. During his talk he confessed his error frankly.

Some of his White House aides, angry at the inept planning and intelligence preparations that had gone into the invasion, tried on their own initiative to fix the blame on the military and intelligence branches. They even charged that Eisenhower, who had begun the invasion project, had been at fault. Characteristically, the President lost no time in setting the record straight. The responsibility had been *his,* not anyone else's, he insisted. Furthermore, he ordered his staff to stop trying to whitewash his failure.

The investigation into the planning blunders connected with the short-lived invasion disclosed some astonishing truths. There had been virtually no communication with rebel groups in Cuba prior to the landing, contrary to what the President had been led to believe. Moreover, the planning for the operation had been carried out by the CIA, with the cooperation of the military leadership, without a real attempt being made to solicit the advice of many of the exile leaders who had been in contact with the Cuban underground.

This, of course, accounted for the mysterious failure of the Cuban insurgents to rise to arms at the time of the landing, and it was now painfully obvious that without adequate air cover, the pitiful little invasion party had never stood a chance.

As a result of the investigation there was a massive shake-up in the nation's top military and intelligence leadership. John R. McCone, former Chairman of the United States Atomic Energy Commission, was appointed to replace Allen Dulles as head of the Central Intelligence Agency.

In the final analysis, the President told himself, the Bay of Pigs had proved to be an expensive lesson that had brought about some concrete reforms. Yet he could not help feeling that from his point of view, the most valuable lesson was his own realization of the awesome responsibility that accompanied the enormous authority of the President of the United States.

13

LIFE IN THE WHITE HOUSE

From the moment that President and Mrs. John F. Kennedy moved into the White House on that frosty day in January of 1961, they discovered that the lives they had led formerly had ceased to exist. In one sense, they were no longer private individuals but symbols of an office—indeed, of a nation.

Nevertheless, they were determined—if only for their children's sake—to maintain as informal an atmosphere as possible at the White House. And they lost no time in setting this new tone in the Executive Mansion.

The first Sunday after they moved into 1600 Pennsylvania Avenue was a quiet, uneventful day. The reporters were in a relaxed mood after the hectic task of covering the events of the previous inauguration week. Suddenly, two familiar figures strolled casually into the Press Room and greeted the newspapermen cheerily. It was the President and Mrs. Kennedy.

An unannounced, informal visit of this type to the Press Room was almost unheard of. The President wore slacks and a sport jacket over a sweater. Mrs. Kennedy was also dressed casually. After they left, the reporters glanced at each other and grinned. Without question this was going to be the most informal White House in history.

The presence of three-year-old Caroline, who habitually wandered throughout the halls of the Executive Mansion, also helped convey the unpretentious mood. One day she entered the Press Room and chatted with the reporters. "What is your daddy doing?" one of them inquired.

"Oh, he's upstairs with his shoes and socks off, doing nothing," the child retorted.

Another time, Mrs. Kennedy was spotted in the halls of the White House wearing her riding breeches, and a tremor of excitement ran through the press corps as its members rushed to their phones to report this bit of intelligence to their newspapers.

Sometimes, the problems of adjusting to the life of Chief Executive were felt by the President in odd ways. A movie fan all his life, he found it difficult, for example, to realize that he could no longer drop in to see a picture whenever he felt like it. One evening, however, he and an aide decided to see *Spartacus,* an adventure film about the revolt of slaves in ancient Rome. Without fanfare, they left the White House and slipped quietly into a neighborhood movie theatre.

In the row of seats just ahead, Kennedy spotted the back of a familiar head. He tapped the man on the shoulder, and a startled Secretary of Agriculture Orville Freeman whirled about to stare into the grinning face of the President of the United States.

"This is one heck of a way to write a farm program," the Chief Executive whispered slyly.

On another occasion during those early months, the President and Mrs. Kennedy planned to dine quietly at the home of Mr. and Mrs. Rowland Evans, Jr., old friends. Evans was a correspondent for the *New York Herald Tribune*. Although only the hosts knew of the impending visit and had not told a soul, the elaborate preparations involved whenever the President goes anywhere were a tip-off. Within a short time almost all of official and semiofficial Washington knew about the visit.

Inevitably, the President and Mrs. Kennedy reluctantly came to the conclusion that their lives would have to be altered in some ways and they might as well resign themselves to it. Because of the responsibilities of the Chief Executive and the traditions associated with his office—including the need to guarantee his safety—he was not and never could be a free agent, at liberty to come and to go everywhere as he pleased. So in the end, the Kennedys fell back on the custom of having friends come to visit them and of seeing their movies at private showings in the White House itself.

Yet in little incidental ways Kennedy continued to find it difficult to adapt himself to his new role. It was established protocol, for instance, for the President to walk a few steps ahead, even when ladies were present, for he is considered to outrank everyone, including his own wife. He found it hard to get used to. Once, the Kennedys received a visit from Mrs. Eleanor Roosevelt. As the widow of the late President Franklin D. Roosevelt, she was far more familiar with presidential protocol than the new First Family. So when the President tried to hold a door open for her, she hung back.

"No, you go first," she told him. "You are the President."

"I keep forgetting," he smiled.

"But you must never forget," the former First Lady replied in a gentle tone.

Though neither he nor other adults were allowed to forget that he was the President of the United States, little Caroline knew him simply as her father. He called her "Buttons" and like millions of other male parents he was required to dream up long, involved bedtime stories for her. When a newspaperman referred to him as "The President" in her presence, little Caroline stamped her foot and protested, "He's not the President, he's my daddy!"

One evening Ambassador Kennedy was talking with his granddaughter long distance. She wanted to speak with her cousin, Steve Smith. Mr. Kennedy could hear in the background the unmistakable voice of his son, the President, pleading, "Hurry up, Caroline, I want to use the phone."

The White House was a sprawling bechive, the nerve center of the executive branch of government. Yet all of its activities were centered about a single large room, the Oval Room, in the west wing of the mansion. This was the President's office. It was where the official business of state was carried out. Here visitors were seen, programs were discussed, legislation was signed.

Dominating one side of the Oval Room was a huge fireplace, and in the fall and winter there was usually a crackling fire dancing on the hearth. On either side of the fireplace were two large couches while on the walls flanking the mantelpiece hung two naval paintings showing scenes in the battle between the immortal American battleship *Constitution* and the British frigate *Guerriere* during the War of 1812. On the mantelpiece itself was a scale model of the *Constitution*. The President worked at a massive ancient desk set in front of the broad windows of the Oval Room, so light could stream in from behind.

From his first day in office, the new Chief Executive found that the long hours of a President's week were filled with work—an endless succession of meetings, thick reports to be read, digested and acted upon, legislative messages to be prepared, speeches to be written. President Kennedy's day began when he was awakened around seven thirty in the morning, but no later than eight. Sometimes he remained in bed to read the newspapers and eat his breakfast, and on other occasions he would gulp down two poached eggs while getting dressed, then go through the papers over coffee.

In recent years, with Mrs. Kennedy's help, he found his taste in clothing running to subdued elegance. He favored tailored, two-button dark or navy blue suits, carefully pressed; white shirts with spread collar; and narrow ties, held by a small, gold alligator tie clasp shaped like a PT-boat. Since he found old footwear comfortable, his black shoes were usually well worn, though burnished so carefully that they gleamed.

At eight thirty or nine, the President would walk to his office, his shoulders hunched forward in thought as he anticipated the problems of the day. His stride was a graceful lope that was rapidly becoming a trademark.

Usually, his work began by reading through the sheaf of messages and memoranda handed to him by Mrs. Evelyn Lincoln, the motherly, gray-haired secretary who had been with him since his senatorial days. Then would come brief, informal conferences with Ted Sorensen, Press Secretary Pierre Salinger or some of his other aides.

Then began the interminable formal meetings and conferences. Not long after he moved into the White House a count was kept of the number of visitors who entered his office on a single day. The total came to

more than one hundred! They included cabinet officers and other high-ranking government executives,
military officials, business and labor leaders, diplomats
and newspaper correspondents, to mention only a few.
A single meeting in the President's office might result in
as many as seventeen separate directives, memoranda
and items of correspondence.

During the first two months of Kennedy's term, he
issued thirty-two official messages and legislative recommendations—his predecessor had issued five during
his first two months in office—to say nothing of twenty-
two Executive Orders and proclamations, and twenty-
eight communications to foreign heads of state. During this same period he also delivered twelve speeches
and held seven press conferences.

To many, the President's working habits seemed
erratic, yet they were an astonishing demonstration of
the efficient channeling of physical and intellectual
energy. While pacing his office or taking a turn around
the corridor, he would read on his feet or dictate to a
secretary with machine-gun rapidity while holding a
conference with one of his aides. Sometimes he would
read and dictate at the same time while strolling back
and forth. On other occasions he would begin a discussion with an assistant or two, then be interrupted by
two or three phone calls or other intrusions, only to return unerringly to the original subject without breaking
mental or verbal stride.

When he was seated, his hands served as the outlet
for his energy. They were rarely still. His fingers would
drum continuously on a matchbook, on the arm of his
chair or even on his teeth.

His reading was phenomenal and included several
books a week in addition to magazines, newspapers

and official material. They included everything—fiction, biography, philosophy and current events. His aides discovered that he read every word of their memoranda. His reading speed ranged from twelve hundred to two thousand words a minute. Staff members soon found that books or magazines were not safe if left out where they could be seen by the "boss" who was an inveterate borrower.

Reporters, too, discovered the President's voracious reading habits. He consumed five newspapers with his breakfast, and sometimes by the time a Washington correspondent reached his office in the morning he would find a telephone message from John F. Kennedy praising or criticizing a particular story he had written for that day's edition.

The President's day rarely ended before seven or eight in the evening. The First Family normally had dinner at eight. But at night there was always a briefcase loaded with presidential "homework," usually reports or other reading matter for which there was no time during the day. One evening, an important report dealing with the political situation in the newly formed Republic of the Congo was rushed to him at ten thirty at night. The report was an inch thick, but by the next morning Kennedy not only had read it but he was prepared to discuss it point by point.

In order to relax and to avoid distractions while writing a speech or other important statement, the President often used the west sitting room of the White House rather than his office. It was a cozy, informal room with furniture which Mrs. Kennedy had had brought over from their previous home. Here, Kennedy would sprawl on a slip-covered couch, scattering reference papers on the floor while writing on a yellow, ruled, legal-length pad.

So heavy was his schedule during those early weeks that on one occasion the President muttered to several of his aides, "Nixon should have won the election." Yet though he felt overburdened and sometimes even frustrated by the endless routine and detail, at the same time he found himself in a state of childlike wonderment. It was as if he could not really accept the fact that he was the President of the United States.

Sometimes he would get up from his desk and begin to poke around the various rooms of the White House, exploring them like a small boy. He would marvel at the sights as if he were one of the thousands of visitors who passed through every year. When he wanted Ted Sorensen or another of his aides, he went searching through the mansion to find him. Often in his eagerness to do and learn everything at once, routine became a shambles.

Nothing was too insignificant to escape his attention. Once he went out on the lawn and noticed crabgrass. Despite all his other burdens, he remembered to instruct a gardener to get rid of it. Always fascinated by the past, he soon mastered the history of many of the pieces of furniture, art and other objects and delighted in relating these facts to friends and visitors.

Mrs. Kennedy, too, was in a state of awe. She had first seen the White House as an eleven-year-old while on a visitors' tour. She remembered the experience vividly. There were moments now when she found it hard to accept the fact that she was now the First Lady of that very same house. Nevertheless, in typically feminine fashion, she also recalled the decorating and furnishing inadequacies. In truth the White House interior was a curious mélange of clashing furniture and bad art that had been donated over the years. One of her first steps was to closet herself with a New York decorator and plan the redecoration of the private quarters of the White House, the rooms where the family would actually live.

She also held conferences with artists, the Director of the National Gallery of Art and the Chairman of the Fine Arts Commission. Soon a grand plan was under way. Mrs. Kennedy was resolved to restore the White House as a historical museum with authentic antiques and tasteful decorating concepts. The work was to be financed by donations—either of money or of pieces of furniture or art. Lorraine Pearce, a specialist in early American history and decorative objects, was brought in and given the title of White House Curator. Her job was to assist the First Lady in refurbishing the Executive Mansion so it would project to the people of America its true historic importance.

The two women undertook a careful search of the White House with its fifty-four rooms and sixteen baths for lost treasures. In an unused room they discovered priceless busts of former Presidents and historic figures like Andrew Jackson, George Washington and Christopher Columbus. A tour of the basement uncovered age-blackened but irreplaceable knives and spoons from Colonial days as well as gold and silver plates dating back to President James Monroe.

Antique furniture of superb craftsmanship was found scattered carelessly everywhere—propped up in a corner of the carpentry shop or gathering dust in the White House storage sheds. Sometimes, as they poked around in long-vacated offices they stumbled across magnificent decorative pieces.

In addition to these discoveries, there was a veritable flood of gifts. Antique collectors from every corner of the land sent in furniture belonging to George Washington, Abraham Lincoln or James Madison. Other donors contributed period draperies, carpets and even wallpaper. The National Gallery of Art also helped, making a loan of paintings by such distinguished American artists as John Singer Sargent and Winslow Homer.

Soon the White House began to undergo a startling transformation. The decorative disarray and confusion of the past gave way to a sense of order and interior design which lent an atmosphere of new dignity and historical significance to the great old mansion. Mrs. Kennedy explained her sense of mission simply. "Before everything slips away," she said, "before every link with the past is gone, I want to do this."

Even before his inauguration the President-Elect had been convinced that few things were as important as the possibility of obtaining a relaxation in the cold war tensions. In his campaign speeches and Inaugural Address he had spoken repeatedly of the need for working for peace. He felt that one of the most significant steps he could take early in his administration was to meet with Soviet Premier Nikita Khrushchev to discuss some of the issues that stood in the way of peaceful negotiation between East and West.

For some time there had been reports of increasing ideological friction between the Soviet Union and Communist China. According to these reports, the Russian leaders believed in "coexistence" with the democracies, so that communism would have time to grow economically strong and eventually dominate the world by peaceful means. The Chinese, on the other hand, reportedly believed that extreme measures, including violence if necessary, should be taken to undermine the Western democracies.

The President reasoned that if the reports of the Russian-Chinese split had any basis in fact, then the Soviet leader might now be willing to resolve some of his differences with the West. Indeed, soon after taking office he had ample reason to strengthen his optimistic view. Four days after his inauguration, the Soviet government informed him through diplomatic channels that they planned to release two imprisoned American Air Force officers, Captains Freeman B. Olmstead and John R. McKone. Seven months earlier, their plane had been shot down by a Soviet fighter in the North Sea, and they had been taken prisoner, charged with violating Russian air space.

The President had made the dramatic announcement of the release of the fliers at his first press conference. It had created a news sensation and had gotten his administration off to a flying start. Many diplomatic observers and commentators had interpreted the Soviet move as a good will gesture toward the new Chief Executive—a sort of inauguration gift. And Kennedy had felt grateful. More important, it had strengthened his belief in the possibility of an eventual summit meeting. Perhaps after six months or so, when he had been in the job for a while and had his feet on the ground, he might take steps to quietly sound out Khrushchev on such a conference.

However, in April came the Bay of Pigs fiasco, and with it went the President's hopes of seeing Khrushchev. The Communist world had leveled severe verbal attacks on the United States. Accordingly, Kennedy now took it for granted that any immediate hope of establishing a dialogue with Nikita Khrushchev to ease the cold war had died on the shores of Cuba as a result of his blundering.

To his complete astonishment, however, diplomatic reports began to trickle through to the White House the following month indicating that a meeting with the Soviet premier was not out of the question after all. The President immediately instructed his aides to encourage such a meeting.

Shortly afterward, the news services began to carry dispatches indicating that in recent speeches Khrushchev had mentioned Kennedy in mild, almost friendly, terms. In the complex language of international diplomacy this was interpreted as a certain clue that Khrushchev favored a meeting. The negotiations continued. Early in June, the Soviet Ambassador, Mikhail Menshikov, appeared at the White House and officially agreed to a meeting between the two heads of state in Vienna on June 4 and 5.

Kennedy had no one specific reason for wanting to meet the Soviet leader. What he did desire was an opportunity to talk with him and study him across a table—to make up his own mind as to the kind of man Khrushchev was. Each international crisis the United States had faced in the past decade and a half had been caused directly or indirectly by the Soviet Union. Kennedy felt it was time to make a new start in trying to ease the tensions that had brought the world close to the brink of war so often for fifteen years.

On the night of May 30, "Air Force One," the official presidential jet—a much larger plane than the private Kennedy plane, the "Caroline"—winged its way across a star-filled sky, headed for Europe. In the cabin, the President sat with Mrs. Kennedy, wondering what his meeting with the Russian premier held in store for the world.

In Paris they were greeted by a crowd of children, some of them Americans carrying little American flags. For the next four days they were entertained lavishly by Premier Charles de Gaulle. Finally, on Saturday morning, June 3, they left France and flew to Vienna.

Khrushchev was already in Austria when they arrived at the Vienna airport. The sky was gray and a light rain was falling as they traveled by motorcade to the residence of the American Ambassador, H. Freeman Matthews. Soon a black Russian automobile purred up to the entrance and Nikita Khrushchev swung his short legs out of the car. The President raced down the stairs to greet him and shake hands.

For the next two days, the two most powerful men on earth talked endlessly. They sparred with words, argued bitterly at times and occasionally found themselves in agreement on a point. Kennedy was now convinced of one thing: Khrushchev was not the buffoon some thought him to be. He knew history thoroughly and could argue Communist philosophy with the expertise of the trained Marxist. No, it would pay to have a healthy respect for this short, bald Russian.

They began to talk about the possibility of a ban on nuclear tests as a first and needed step toward peace. Khrushchev reiterated Russian support for immediate and total disarmament without provisions for inspections inside a country's borders by an international body. Once disarmament took place and the capitalist countries proved their honorable intentions, he indicated, then and only then would the Russians be willing to discuss inspections.

President Kennedy, on the other hand, underscored

the importance of getting some sort of limited agreement with inspection of safeguards, if only as an important first step in overcoming the mutual distrust that now stood as a barrier to any sort of treaty. To illustrate his point, he cited an old Chinese proverb: "The journey of a thousand miles begins with one step."

Khrushchev seemed startled at his familiarity with the saying. "You seem to know the Chinese very well," he remarked.

"We may both get to know them better," the President retorted in a wry allusion to the reports of Soviet-Chinese acrimony.

Khrushchev was particularly smitten with lovely Mrs. Kennedy who sat next to him at a huge state dinner. The Premier edged his chair closer to her so he could converse more easily.

The final conversations between Khrushchev and Kennedy were about Soviet-American differences over Berlin. Since the end of World War II, Berlin had stood as a thorn in the side of the Communist world. After the war a four-power command—United States, Russia, England and France—had been agreed upon to govern the city which was in the heart of Communist East Germany. By 1948 disagreements between East and West had destroyed the four-power command, and Berlin was split in two, with the Communists controlling the East portion and the democracies the West portion of the city.

West Berlin now became an island of freedom in Communist-ruled Eastern Germany. Hundreds of thousands of East Germans fled to West Berlin to escape Communist oppression. Berlin became such a propaganda liability for the Communist world that the

Soviet leadership had continuously threatened to cut off Western access to the city which was guaranteed under the original agreement. The democracies had warned the Communist leaders that any step to sever the West's access corridor to West Berlin would violate the post-World War II treaty and might lead to war.

Khrushchev now repeated the familiar diatribe against West Berlin, arguing that geographically it was an unnatural wart on the face of East Germany and the West could not expect it to remain separate from East Germany forever. President Kennedy replied that the West was in Berlin legally and would use force to maintain its rights there, at any risk. By now the discussion had become rancorous, and it was on this unfortunate note that they parted.

In all, their conversations had totaled eleven hours. Nevertheless, in spite of his failure to persuade the Russian leader to change even a few of his ideas, the President felt that the meeting had been invaluable. He now knew exactly where Khrushchev stood on important issues, and this knowledge would be helpful in determining America's policies in the future.

14

THE NEW FRONTIER

For the Kennedys the months seemed to fly by now. Life was a round of meetings, speeches, official functions and good will tours, in addition to the heavy schedule of routine work in the White House.

Of late, however, the President had learned to lean heavily on Vice-President Lyndon Johnson as his personal representative on many good will missions—although he himself continued to participate in the most important ones. The tall Texan had proved to be a stalwart prop on whom he could depend implicitly for political astuteness and sound administrative judgment.

During one groundbreaking ceremony in Canada, the President shoveled a spadeful of dirt and succeeded in aggravating his old back trouble. Dr. Janet Travell continued giving him massive injections of pain-killing drugs. She also prescribed a rocking chair for his office and a light corset to support his back. To get around in the White House, he began to use crutches, although he discarded them in public. Yet in spite of the pain, which even the injections could not deaden entirely, he continued to observe a full schedule.

In late fall, the President and Mrs. Kennedy went on

a tour of South America. It was a good will effort, planned in order to help the Alliance for Progress. It proved to be a great success.

Throughout South America they appeared before massed crowds, speaking directly to faces pinched with poverty and lined with despair. Once, Mrs. Kennedy stood in a Venezuelan farmyard surrounded by poor peasants. She was wearing an expensive dress and coat of apricot-colored linen and silk, and yet they did not seem to resent her for she was speaking to them in Spanish, telling them things they could understand.

"We will be more than good neighbors," she told them. "We will be partners in building a better life for our peoples. No fathers or mothers can be happy until they have the possibility of jobs and education for their children. This must be for all and not just a few."

Her small audience nodded in quiet understanding. She had spoken simple words that had reached their hearts. How surprising it was that this great lady from America to the north knew how to talk to them in ways that they could readily comprehend.

It was that way all through South America. Everywhere they were given warm greetings, and hands of friendship were extended to them as sincere ambassadors of good will from the United States.

President and Mrs. Kennedy had barely returned to Washington when there was bad news. An urgent telephone call from Palm Beach informed him that his father had suffered a severe stroke. Dazed and worried, he flew down to Florida to remain at the Ambassador's side. At last the doctors announced that he was out of danger. Although Mr. Kennedy would survive, they told the President, he would be permanently impaired.

While the President's first year in office had brought few solutions to the long-range problems besetting the country, there was no disputing the First Family's personal impact on the nation.

It suddenly seemed that every woman in the country wanted to look like Jacqueline Kennedy. Overnight, her bouffant hairdo had become the rage, and the fashion pages of the slick magazines featured models who looked enough like the First Lady to be her twin.

The President's influence was no less dramatic. New Frontier had become the expression that symbolized youth, vigor, determination and dedication. His own aides sometimes found themselves picking up certain characteristics of their boss. The pointed forefinger, the emphatic gesture of the hands palm down—these became occupational mannerisms of the "new frontiersmen."

In truth, a new way of life had come to staid Washington. It was a combination of cultural and intellectual pursuits tempered with a vigorous routine of swimming, golf, tennis and touch football.

Sometimes this emulation of the First Family took an unusual turn. When word had spread that the President was able to read twelve hundred words a minute, there was a rush to enroll in speed reading courses, and teachers had to be imported into the capital. Dining at home, a favorite form of relaxation for the Kennedys, suddenly replaced lavish restaurant dining as a social ritual, to the irritation of restaurant owners.

The New Frontier was also symbolized by the presence of lots of children. The Kennedy administration was composed of young people, many with small sons and daughters. There were seventeen youngsters in the Kennedy clan alone. A small school was established in the White House for Caroline and the younger children of other administration personnel. Members of the White House staff soon grew accustomed to the noise of laughing and shouting children echoing through the hallowed corridors of the Executive Mansion. For the President, the presence of Caroline and baby John served as a tonic that never failed to lift his spirits, even when affairs of state weighed heavily on his shoulders.

Sometimes Caroline would burst into his office while he was in the midst of an important conference and demand attention. No matter how busy he was, Kennedy never failed to take time out to attend to her problem of the moment. During the day, he made it a practice to take a few minutes out to see his son—the President lovingly referred to him as John-John—while the tot was being fed or bathed. In spite of the tremendous demands on his time and energy, he found that being President actually allowed him to spend more time with his family than when he had been a Senator constantly on the campaign trail.

Because of the insatiable public interest in all the activities of the Kennedy family, the newspapers had a field day. A newsman would spot Caroline and her friends playing on the White House lawn, and this was worth a dispatch. Mrs. Kennedy would be seen water skiing, and the next day front pages across the country would carry a three-column photograph. If the President was observed hitting a golf ball near the White House fence, it was news. So completely did the activities of the Kennedys dominate the news media that occasionally truly important events were overshadowed, much to the President's exasperation. At times, for example, he wanted to bring an important matter of legislation or foreign policy to the attention of the people, only to find that the press was more interested in Macaroni, Caroline's pony.

During the campaign for the Presidency, Kennedy had complained to audiences that he was "tired of getting up every morning and reading in my newspaper what Khrushchev and Castro are doing. What I want is to awake and see headlines about what the President of the United States is doing."

One morning, Ted Sorensen entered the Oval Room waving a newspaper with the front page heavily weighted with Kennedy headlines. "People," he declared impishly, "are tired of waking up every morning and reading what Kennedy is doing. They want to know what Khrushchev and Castro are doing."

Privacy for the First Family was virtually nonexistent. Even when the press was not around, there was still the cordon of Secret Service agents whose job it was to guard the President and his family.

Kennedy's own view of the Presidency had broadened during his first year in office. He now saw that the influence of the Chief Executive was enormous, not only in matters of government, but in other areas as well. For example, he had viewed with amazement the tendency of the American people to emulate the First Family in their habits of dress and their activities. It gave him a stunning idea. If the President and his lady were able to exert leadership in matters of fashion, why couldn't they use their tremendous influence to improve the quality of American life as well? Was there anything to prevent them from stimulating greater interest in art and culture? American society was a good society. With proper encouragement it might develop into a brilliant civilization. Greece had had its Golden

Age. Why couldn't America be blessed with a similar era?

President and Mrs. Kennedy had long discussions on the subject and made bold plans. They spoke about bringing fine concerts and ballets and even operas to the White House. With Mrs. Kennedy as producer and casting director, a bright new page could be written in American culture!

One of the first of these presentations featured the National Symphony Orchestra, brought in to play at a specially erected pavilion on the White House lawn, following a state dinner to President Mohammed Ayub Kahn of Pakistan. So successful was the affair that Mrs. Kennedy followed it with recitals by opera stars Roberta Peters and Jerome Hines. At other times there were scenes and excerpts by players from the American Shakespeare Festival Theatre; a program of Elizabethan poetry—with music—read by film and stage star Basil Rathbone; and a reading of American prose excerpts by Frederic March. The audience for this last presentation was a gathering of all the Nobel Prize Winners of the Western Hemisphere, who had been especially invited to the White House to spend an evening with "Jack and Jackie."

Then, the First Lady scored a brilliant triumph as impresario. The world-famous cellist, Pablo Casals, was induced to come to the Executive Mansion to perform in honor of Governor Muñoz-Marin of Puerto Rico. Casals, a refugee from Spain since the time of the Spanish Revolution in the 1930's, had sworn never to play in any country that recognized the dictatorship of General Francisco Franco, but at the request of the President, he broke his pledge and agreed to give a concert. The story made the front pages of newspapers throughout the world.

For the children there was a series of "Concerts for Young People by Young People," which brought folk singers and dancers and musicians—both classical and jazz—to the White House. Mrs. Kennedy shared the President's strong feelings about the importance of encouraging American cultural interests and taste, particularly among children. It was for that reason that she put extraordinary effort into the task of redecorating and refurbishing the White House.

She explained her view to a visitor this way: "My mother brought me to Washington one Easter when I was eleven. That was the first time I saw the White House. From the outside I remember the feeling of the place. But inside all I remember was shuffling through. They didn't point anything out. They didn't even give you a booklet telling you about it. I didn't remember anything specific." Then, after a pause, she added thoughtfully, "I want every little boy who goes through this White House to get some sense of history, to be shown things and have them explained. But I also want it esthetic. Girls must go out and make homes, and I want it to seem not only significant but to give them a sense of beauty so they will be inspired in their jobs."

As the Kennedys' second winter in the White House drew to an end, Washington got ready to celebrate its annual Cherry Blossom Festival. April 10, 1962, was a sunny spring day. Out on the rear lawn of the White House, little Caroline prepared to exercise her pony Macaroni while Mrs. Kennedy watched. Inside the mansion, the President worked quietly in his office. It was an uneventful day with no more than the usual minor crises to contend with.

In midafternoon there was a call from Roger Blough, chairman of the United States Steel Corporation, who requested to see the President later that day. The appointment was made. Blough was the spokesman for the steel industry.

For some months the President and Arthur Goldberg, the Secretary of Labor, had been involved in negotiations between the steel companies and the labor unions on a new contract. The steelworkers wanted a sizable increase in wages. Kennedy knew that if the steel companies granted the wage increase and raised the price of steel to cover the added labor costs, it would lead to a general inflation which would give the nation's economy a body blow. Therefore, he had Secretary Goldberg—himself a former counsel for the steelworkers' union—to use his influence to talk the unions into modifying their demands. They did. The steel workers scaled their requests down so drastically that an analysis of cost-price factors showed that no increase would be required. Blough and the other executives seemed satisfied. The President congratulated both sides for their statesmanship, while the press of the country hailed the administration's feat as a triumph for the national interest.

When Blough showed up at the White House late in the afternoon he and the President greeted each other in friendly fashion. Kennedy waved him to the couch while he himself sat in his rocking chair.

The steel spokesman handed the Chief Executive a news release. It announced that the United States Steel Corporation was raising the price of steel six dollars a ton! Kennedy was so amazed that for a long moment he didn't know quite what to say. "I think you're making a mistake," he told Blough at last in a grim voice.

After the United States Steel chairman left, his anger grew. Almost immediately, there were bulletins that the other big steel companies had followed Blough's lead and raised their prices, at which point the President realized that he had been the victim of a giant hoax. The steel companies had deceived the steel workers, the public and even the President. His prestige and hence that of the American government was at stake. The steel companies were powerful, but they must be taught that they were not more important or more powerful than the people of the United States, he told himself.

All that night and the next morning, the President, Vice-President Johnson and aides worked out their strategy. In the afternoon, the President was scheduled to appear at his regular press conference, so it was agreed that he should use the meeting with the reporters as the occasion to reply to the steel companies' challenge.

Ted Sorensen and the President worked carefully on a prepared statement. On the way over to the new State Department Auditorium where the conference was to be held, Kennedy read and reread the statement until he knew it almost by heart.

As he walked out before the assembled newsmen he was tight-lipped and unsmiling. There was not a sound in the room. Without any preliminaries, he proceeded to read his statement in measured tones. It was a blistering attack on the perfidy of the steel executives such as few of those assembled had ever heard before. He slowed up at certain parts to give added emphasis to his words: ". . . the American people will find it hard, as I do, to accept a situation in which a tiny handful of steel executives, whose pursuit of power and profit exceeds their sense of public responsibility, can show such utter contempt for the interests of one hundred and eighty-five million Americans. . . ." Later he stalked off, anger still mirrored in his face.

The headlines in the late afternoon and morning papers were eloquent testimony to the power of the presidential office. Even papers unfriendly to the administration featured the President's statement on their front pages because it was news.

Public response was immediate and favorable. From every corner of the nation telegrams and telephone messages of support poured in. Now it was the American people speaking, backing their President's action overwhelmingly. At a White House meeting with his aides, Kennedy came in with an armful of telegrams. "We're way ahead," he said, grinning for the first time since his meeting with Blough.

The presidential offensive against the price increase mounted in intensity. A Navy defense order for steel plate which was supposed to go to United States Steel was given instead to Lukens Steel Company which had not raised its prices. Inland Steel, one of the nation's largest independent producers, whose officials were friendly with some of the President's aides, agreed not to raise prices, at least for the next two weeks.

Toward the end of the week, organized steel began to crack. One of the companies, Bethlehem, announced it was rescinding the price increase! Less than two hours later, Roger Blough's United States Steel followed. All the other companies immediately fell into line.

Much of the press had been in favor of the President's course of action and congratulated him on his victory. Some of the more conservative newspapers accused him of using excessive pressure in routing the steel companies. They charged him with being "anti-business." But the President knew from the mail that had come in that the American people had supported him fully; and in any case, he told himself, he had done the right thing for the country.

Even when there were successes, like that in the steel crisis, there was little time for self-congratulations. For a President there were always new problems to be faced. Sometimes several crises developed simultaneously.

Kennedy soon realized that one of the most nagging and difficult problems would have to do with civil rights. Already civil rights controversies were brewing in various parts of the South as Negroes, after a century of oppression, were beginning to make their demands for equality felt.

In the summer of 1962, Kennedy and his aides began to prepare for trouble in Mississippi. Word had been received that a twenty-nine-year-old Negro student and Air Force veteran, James Meredith, would seek enrollment for the fall term at the University of Mississippi. The institution, known as Ole Miss, was a state-supported university and thus subject to the Supreme Court desegregation decisions. Ole Miss had never had a Negro, and for this reason Meredith decided to offer himself as a test case.

Mississippi was one of the most militantly segregationist states in the South. Its governor, Ross Barnett, had defied the Supreme Court decision and ordered the university to refuse to enroll Meredith. Thus encouraged by the top political leader of the state, segregationist groups, aided by agitators from outside who poured into Mississippi, vowed to fight to the bitter end to prevent integration at Ole Miss.

The President and Attorney-General Kennedy were painfully aware of the possibility of violence. The Justice Department was instructed to have federal marshals available to escort the Negro student to the campus.

As the threat of bloodshed grew, Barnett, awakened at last to the potential bombshell he had set off, was frightened. He promised the Justice Department to have enough state troopers on hand to prevent disorder. The President and Bobby Kennedy, however, wondered whether the governor would have the political courage to use his state police against mobs of white Mississippians if serious trouble did develop.

On Sunday, October 2, James Meredith arrived at the Ole Miss campus in Oxford, Mississippi, to seek the rights which the Constitution of the United States guaranteed him as a citizen. He was accompanied by a platoon of marshals and state troopers. A huge mob had formed, but at the crucial moment, when it appeared that there would be trouble, the state troopers walked off, leaving the marshals to handle the mob alone. Soon the shouts and jeers grew into violence. The mob surged forth onto the campus.

Thoroughly shaken by the explosion his demagoguery had sparked, Governor Barnett frantically called Washington to say that he could not protect Meredith and to plead that the Negro student be removed from the campus for his own safety. The President was furious. He warned that he would discuss nothing until Barnett did his duty and took steps to enforce the law. "There are lives in jeopardy," the Chief Executive shouted into the phone angrily. "I'm not in a position to do anything, make any deals, to discuss anything until law and order is restored and the lives of the people are protected. Good-by." He slammed down the receiver.

In Oxford, a full-scale riot had broken out on the Ole Miss campus. The federal marshals tried to ward off the crowd with tear gas, but with no state troopers around, they were so completely outnumbered that controlling the mob was out of the question. Soon a battle ensued in which a French newspaperman and one of the rioters were killed by small-arms fire.

The President decided not to wait any longer. He ordered federal troops into Oxford. By five thirty in the morning, when he wearily decided to go to bed, the rioters had been dispersed and the situation was under control at last.

Meredith had been enrolled.

The President regretted the loss of life and the damage to university property, but he knew that he had done what had to be done. If American democracy was to have any meaning at all, the United States government must be prepared to use the full extent of its power—even fixed bayonets, if necessary—to guarantee that a Negro would have the same rights as any other citizen.

Barely had the crisis in Mississippi been quelled when the President found himself with a new international dilemma on his hands. Once again Cuba was the central point in the drama.

For a number of weeks, the Central Intelligence Agency had received reports from informants inside Cuba that Russian-made ballistic missiles were being installed on the island. Early in the morning of October 14, an American plane was dispatched to make a

211

reconnaissance run over the suspected areas. The photographs from the plane's cameras were sharp and clear. They definitely confirmed the intelligence reports: medium-range missiles of Russian origin had been installed in Cuba. A report was rushed to the President in Washington. He was profoundly shocked. Soviet missiles ninety miles from the United States could only mean that Khrushchev was taking a desperate gamble. Clearly, he was hoping to change the military power balance in the belief that the United States would not dare stand up against such an aggressive move for fear of starting a nuclear war. For Kennedy, the challenge was obvious. Either he would have to ignore the Soviet maneuver, thus opening the way to future Russian actions against the United States, or else he would have to stand up to Khrushchev by demanding that he remove the missiles or take the consequences!

The President saw that in reality he had no choice. No matter how risky and dangerous, he knew he would have to get tough with the Russians.

The rest of that week was spent in careful checking, rechecking and planning. Having confirmed the accuracy of the reconnaissance photos and their interpretation, he now concerned himself with the mode of action. The Russians would have to be confronted, but how? Moreover, what strategy should the United States follow to make certain that the flow of missiles to Cuba was cut off?

The lights in the White House burned late as the President met with Vice-President Lyndon Johnson, Defense Secretary Robert McNamara, U.N. Ambassador Adlai Stevenson, Ted Sorensen and other aides to discuss the situation. At last a plan of action was agreed upon. They would institute a *blockade*. The United States Navy would quarantine Cuba and search incoming ships for missile cargoes. It was daring and courageous, for a blockade was in reality an act of war. Yet, if it were to remain the champion of the free world, the United States had no alternative.

Still acutely conscious of the bungled Bay of Pigs affair, the President had no intention of repeating his earlier mistake. Each tactical detail was questioned closely, scrutinized and checked once more before he approved its inclusion in the over-all plan of action.

So far, the American people were unaware of what was happening. Now, the President decided, the time had come to let them in on the crisis. Late in the afternoon of Monday, October 22, he sent a copy of a carefully prepared speech to the Russian Ambassador with the notation that the address would be delivered that night over television.

The networks had cooperated in making preparations for a special broadcast. The President felt calmer than he had expected as air time neared. Finally the moment arrived; he was given the signal to begin speaking.

"Good evening, my fellow citizens . . ."

He told the nation about the missile buildup and about the danger of nuclear war. Then he spoke of the quarantine, which had two goals: "To prevent the use of these missiles against this or any other country and to secure their withdrawal or elimination from the Western Hemisphere." He added, "It shall be the policy of this nation to regard any nuclear missile launched from Cuba against any nation in the Western Hemisphere as an attack by the Soviet Union on the United States requiring a full retaliatory response upon the

Soviet Union." Finally: "The cost of freedom is always high but Americans have always paid it."

Now it was up to Khrushchev. Soviet ships would have to stop and submit to search or be attacked. While a tense nation and world waited, Russian ships headed for Cuba.

In the White House, the presidential staff was swamped by letters and telegrams indicating support for the Chief Executive's bold and determined action. The press was almost unanimous in its support, too.

On Friday, October 26, a Russian chartered Lebanese freighter was stopped by two American destroyers, one of them ironically named the USS *Joseph P. Kennedy, Jr.*, after the President's older brother. The Soviet vessel did not resist. She was boarded and searched and found to be carrying sulphur, paper and trucks. As a result, she was allowed to proceed to Cuba.

Russia did nothing about it.

In the war of nerves, the President had triumphed. Khrushchev had gambled and lost, and in the process he had suffered a humiliating defeat.

Having won the battle to prevent more missiles from entering Cuba, Kennedy now proceeded to concern himself with those already there. He sent the Soviet Premier a letter demanding that he have the Cuban missiles dismantled and removed. On October 29, Khrushchev agreed to this course of action. The entire world breathed a sigh of relief. The President issued a statement at once, hailing the Russian move. It read: "I welcome Chairman Khrushchev's statesmanlike decision to stop building bases in Cuba, to dismantle offensive weapons and return them to the Soviet Union under United Nations verification. This is an important constructive contribution to peace. . . .

It is my earnest hope that the governments of the world can, with a solution to the Cuban crisis, turn their earnest attention to the compelling necessities for ending the arms race and reducing world tensions."

Overnight, the President's stature among the American people and the peoples of the world had risen enormously. He had faced a critical test of nerves and skill, one that had brought the world close to the brink of war, and he had passed it superbly. For the first time he felt that he had made at least partial amends to the nation for the humiliating Bay of Pigs blunder.

The Cuban blockade had resulted in an additional dividend—it had indicated to Kennedy that Khrushchev was as horrified by the prospect of nuclear war as the leaders of the Western nations. If so, then perhaps the dialogue he had established with the Soviet Premier in Vienna the previous year could be revived. Was it possible that the near-tragedy of the past few weeks had actually set the stage for an important step toward world peace? he asked himself.

As the fall of 1962 gave way to winter, the President felt more assured and relaxed than at any time in the past. He felt at last he had the solid trust and support of the American people. Although he was barely halfway through his term, the public opinion polls indicated that if he were to run for re-election, he would be returned to office by a landslide.

Shortly after the beginning of the New Year, the President received a surprisingly cordial letter from Premier Nikita Khrushchev. It read, in part, "The time has come now to put an end once and for all to nuclear tests. We are ready to meet you halfway."

For many months negotiators from seventeen nations had been meeting in Geneva, Switzerland, to discuss precisely this issue, yet they had made no headway. Consequently, the President was delighted to receive word that Khrushchev was serious about negotiating an agreement. What's more, the Soviet leader's proposal included a ban that would provide for two or three inspections of suspicious tremors each year, to prevent "cheating."

In the past, it had been the issue of inspections that had served as a roadblock to any sort of agreement with the Russians. The United States had demanded an inspection system, the Communists had vehemently opposed it. Khrushchev's offer, then, represented a major concession. The President sent word to American negotiators in Geneva that he felt the Russians were ready to talk business. The disarmament talks resumed on a new note of optimism.

Less than two months later, on April 5, 1963, Kennedy received a second surprise from Premier Khrushchev. The Soviet leader sent a message indicating that he was interested in installing a direct line Teletype system between Washington and Moscow. It would be a private communications line that would remain open and ready for use at an instant's notice any time of the day or night.

For over a year, political experts had advocated such a "hot line" so that in case of a sudden crisis, communications between the two countries would be continuous and immediate. Until now, the procedure had been to use commercial telegraph, often with delays of hours before messages were received. The interest shown by Khrushchev in installing a "hot line" was significant, for he had shown little predisposition in favor of such a proposal when it had been suggested by American diplomats to Soviet representatives. The

President interpreted the new move as further evidence of the Russian Premier's desire to encourage a thaw in the cold war. Accordingly, he instructed the American disarmament negotiators in Switzerland to follow through on the "hot line" issue at once with the Soviet representatives there.

In spite of the demanding tasks before him, the President found time to enjoy his children more than before. At five and a half, Caroline was turning into a little lady, and two-and-a-half-year-old John-John was developing a personality of his own. The children liked nothing better than to barge in during an important conference and demand that their father play with them. John-John loved to cup his tiny hand around the President's ear and buzz into it, as if confiding some vital state secret. His father would nod thoughtfully and say, "My, my. You don't say," and the little boy would burst out laughing. It was a game John-John never grew tired of playing.

Sometimes, when the Chief Executive had a few free minutes, the children would come into the Oval Room and perform a little dance they had learned, while he kept time by clapping his hands.

All children seemed to love him. Occasionally he would step out into the White House rose garden and clap his hands, and Caroline and John-John and every other child and dog within earshot would come running.

For relaxation, the President and Mrs. Kennedy continued to hold small intimate parties for writers, artists and show people at the White House. But often, late at night, before going to sleep, the President would play records. One of the songs he enjoyed was from the Broadway musical, *Camelot*. The lines he loved most were: *Don't let it be forgot, that once there was a spot, for one brief shining moment that was known as Camelot.*

The song brought back memories of his own childhood when, sick in bed, he had read about the Knights of the Round Table and Ivanhoe and other heroes of old, both real and legendary. And he could not help thinking how marvelous it would be if the illusions and ideals of childhood could shine permanently instead of tarnishing with the passage of time.

15

TRAGEDY IN TEXAS

To his aides, the President seemed more at ease than ever before.

His perspective seemed to have broadened, so that each daily problem of the presidential office no longer was treated as a life-and-death crisis. In truth, he had learned the virtue of not taking himself too seriously.

His wit was more in evidence, too—an added sign of his increasing self-assurance. Once, complaining about Congress' refusal to pass needed legislation, he remarked wryly, "I never realized how powerful the Senate was until I left it and came up to this end of Pennsylvania Avenue." Another time, Kennedy, who was notoriously poor in foreign languages, began an address to an audience of Latin Americans, "After some debate and protest, it was decided that I would *not* make the speech in Spanish!"

Early in the spring, Mrs. Kennedy learned that she was going to have a baby in the late summer. The President was jubilant. The announcement was carried in front page headlines across the nation.

There were other reasons for satisfaction, too. The Peace Corps had confounded all its critics by turning into one of the nation's most successful foreign ventures. It had made firm friends all over the world and had even won the admiration of Congress. In addition, Kennedy received word that the test-ban negotiations with Russia were going so well that there was solid reason to hope that an agreement would soon be reached.

However, on the civil rights front, things were as tense as ever. In early May, racial demonstrations broke out in Birmingham, Alabama. The city was under the domination of a Public Safety Commissioner, Eugene "Bull" Connor, a brutal last-ditch segregationist who had intimidated the Negro populace for more than two decades.

Under the leadership of Dr. Martin Luther King, Jr. the Negroes of Birmingham had decided at last to stand up for their rights. They organized freedom parades and demonstrations to demand the desegregation of schools, restaurants and other facilities. Connor ordered his policemen to use high-pressure hoses and police dogs against the freedom marchers. Pictures of dogs ripping the clothes off frightened Negroes were displayed to a shocked world in newspapers throughout the United States and abroad.

Horrified by the treatment accorded the marchers by the Birmingham officials, the President instructed the Attorney-General to send a Justice Department team to the beleaguered city. The government representatives succeeded in working out an agreement between the Negro community and a "citizens' committee" which had been organized by some of the more moderate businessmen and civic leaders who feared for Birmingham's welfare. The agreement provided for increased civil rights for Negroes.

When an uneasy peace had been restored, the President decided that the moment had arrived for drastic action on a national level. He announced that he would press to have a comprehensive civil rights bill passed by Congress to provide Negroes with the rights of citizenship guaranteed them under the Constitution.

The provisions of the bill would, among other things, provide equal access for Negroes in all places of "public accommodation" such as hotels, restaurants and retail stores. The legislation would also authorize the Attorney-General of the United States to sue against public school segregation when Negroes affected presented a written complaint to the Justice Department. In the past many Negroes in the South could not afford the expense of bringing private lawsuits in segregation cases or feared reprisals. Finally, the civil rights bill would simplify and strengthen the legal procedures already in existence used to assure job equality and voting rights for Negroes.

On June 11, the President delivered a report to the American people on the civil rights crisis:

> Now the time has come for this nation to fulfill its promise. The events in Birmingham and elsewhere have so increased the cries for equality that no city or state or legislative body can prudently choose to ignore them. . . . It is time to act in the Congress, in your state and local legislative body, and, above all, in all our daily lives.

Thus, although controversy and violence continued to flare up in many American communities, the struggle of the Negroes was at last being dramatized through a comprehensive piece of legislation. The South, of course, voiced strong opposition to the bill.

Southern Congressmen threatened to fight it with every legislative trick at their command. Yet the President was confident of ultimate victory, for he was entirely convinced that judgment of time and history were on his side—on the side of equality for all Americans.

On the nuclear test-ban front, the summer of 1963 was proving even more significant than had been expected. Having received word that a limited treaty was definitely possible, Kennedy sent Undersecretary of State Averell Harriman, a former Ambassador to Moscow, to the Soviet Union to complete top-level negotiations.

It was now apparent that Khrushchev was sincere in his avowed desire for a test-ban agreement. Harriman, a diplomat with superb experience in dealing with the Russians, and Viscount Hailsham, representing Great Britain, sat down with the Soviet Premier who declared heartily, "We begin immediately with the signing."

In spite of the fact that Soviet and American diplomats had negotiated for years without success, it now took only a matter of days to work out the details for a treaty. The discussions bogged down on only one point—the old issue of inspections. Khrushchev, in his letter to Kennedy, had offered to go along with two or three. Harriman, on instructions from the President, held out for six or seven. Khrushchev offered to allow monitoring stations in Russia to supplement the on-site inspections, but Harriman's scientific advisers pointed out that the locations which Khrushchev offered would be practically valueless.

A compromise was needed. Both the Russian and American scientists agreed that nuclear testing above ground, which was responsible for poisoning the atmosphere with "atomic fallout," could be detected anywhere on earth with existing scientific apparatus. So could detonations in outer space or under water. It was only *underground* nuclear explosions which could not be detected at a distance and for which on-site inspections were needed. Rather than have the negotiations break down, Khrushchev and Harriman agreed to exclude underground nuclear testing from the present test-ban agreement, but to leave the matter open for future negotiation.

At the same time, progress was being made in Geneva. The American and Russian delegates to the disarmament conference there reached a comprehensive agreement for the "hot line" between Washington and Moscow. The plan called for the "hot line" to become operational on August 30, 1963.

Although he had been prepared for encouraging developments, the President could hardly believe the momentous news from Europe. For the first time in years the path to peace had been opened up. True, the limited test-ban treaty would not resolve all conflict between the United States and Russia; there would be new problems, new challenges and new dangers as time went on. Nevertheless, when all was said and done, the treaty stood as a historic landmark in the quest for a peaceful world.

On July 26, the President reported to the nation on the test-ban treaty. In his address, he repeated the saying he had once recited for Khrushchev's benefit:

According to the ancient Chinese proverb, "a journey of a thousand miles must begin with a single step." My fellow Americans, let us take that first step. Let us, if we can, step back from the shadows of war and seek out the way of peace.

And if that journey is a thousand miles or even more, let history record that we, in this land, at this time, took the first step.

The American people listened and approved. Editorials hailed the agreement. And so did the United States Senate which, after eleven days of formal debate, confirmed the treaty. For Kennedy it was one of the most important moments of his Presidency.

As the summer of 1963 wore on, there was time for relaxation—for swimming and sailing at Hyannis Port as in the old days—and some quiet hours for reflection. Even the President's back seemed to have improved, so that he was able to take up golf again, a game he had not played for several years.

Toward the end of August the pleasant sequence was suddenly interrupted by a sad interlude. Although Mrs. Kennedy had not been expecting the birth of their baby for another few weeks, she began to have pain, was rushed to the hospital where she gave birth prematurely.

The baby turned out to be a son, only four pounds ten ounces. They christened him Patrick Bouvier Kennedy. But there were complications. The infant was suffering from a breathing blockage. For thirty-nine hours the doctors worked frantically to keep him alive, but their efforts were useless. A grim-faced Pierre Salinger had to issue the following statement to the press: "Patrick Kennedy died at 4:04 A.M. The struggle of the baby boy to keep breathing was too much for his heart."

Baby Patrick was placed in a small white casket in which the President had placed a gold St. Christopher's medal which his wife had once given him. Richard Cardinal Cushing read a Mass of the Holy Angels, and then the child was buried in a family plot in Brookline.

The President and Mrs. Kennedy grieved. The nation grieved with them. Yet in spite of a heavy heart, Kennedy continued to attend to his duties, for he knew that even deep personal sorrow must not be allowed to interfere with the work of the President.

With the coming of autumn, domestic and foreign affairs seemed more settled than they had been in months. The President turned his thoughts to his political prospects for the future. While the presidential election was still a year away, he decided that it was not too soon to begin laying groundwork for the campaign. After all, his success in 1960 had stemmed from careful early planning. And while the public opinion polls showed that his re-election was virtually assured, he decided to leave nothing to chance.

After strategy meetings with brother Bobby, Ted Sorensen and the others, he decided that preliminary campaigning would be wise. Particularly in the South, where the rumblings of discontent over the civil rights issue were being heard. He felt that a trip through several of the southern states would afford an excellent chance to sense the mood of the people, for he knew from experience that secondhand reports—no matter how detailed and carefully prepared—were no substitute for personal contact with the voters themselves. Consequently it was agreed that he and Mrs. Kennedy would visit Florida and Texas.

A light rain blanketed Fort Worth on the morning of November 22, 1963. Bareheaded and coatless, the President left his hotel and strode across the street to a parking lot where a large crowd of people had gathered to catch a glimpse of him. He was in excellent spirits, for the campaigning in Florida had gone well, much better than he had expected. In fact, he was beginning to believe that the experts who claimed he had lost the support of the entire South because of his strong stand on civil rights may have been overly hasty in their judgment.

In the parking lot he began to shake hands with a few of the thousands of Texans who had massed behind a rope barricade to greet him enthusiastically. They were cheerful and friendly—further confirmation that it might have been premature to write off the South.

"Where is Mrs. Kennedy?" a man shouted good-naturedly.

The President grinned. "Mrs. Kennedy is busy organizing herself," he replied. "It takes a little longer, you know, but then she looks so much better than we do." The crowd laughed delightedly.

Two hours later, President and Mrs. Kennedy boarded "Air Force One" for the next stop on their itinerary—Dallas. Some of the White House advisers had objected to his going to Texas, a state that was a haven for a number of right wing extremist groups. Just four weeks earlier, UN Ambassador Adlai Stevenson had been struck with a placard and spat upon by right wing pickets after a speech in Dallas. Nevertheless, the President felt the trip was important enough for him to risk the possibility of an unpleasant incident.

The presidential plane landed at Love Field near Dallas a little after eleven thirty. A group of greeters presented Mrs. Kennedy with a colorful bouquet of flowers. After an official ceremony at the airfield, the

President and First Lady, accompanied by Texas Governor John Connally and his wife, were escorted to the Chief Executive's big blue Lincoln convertible for the ten-mile ride through Dallas to the city's Trade Mart where they were to attend a civic lunch. Also in the party were Vice-President and Mrs. Johnson who were to ride in another automobile in the twelve-car motorcade.

Unlike Fort Worth, the weather in Dallas was perfect. A bright, warm sun was shining, so the President decided to dispense with the car's bubble top canopy. As the motorcade slowly made its way along the route, great crowds of people lined the roadway ten and twelve deep. The reception was every bit as enthusiastic as the one they had received in Fort Worth.

Mrs. Connally, an attractive, vivacious woman, turned to Kennedy and said, "Well, Mr. President, you can't say Dallas doesn't love you."

He grinned and continued to wave to the throngs of admirers. Now they were only two miles from their destination, cruising along the expressway at fifteen miles an hour. Up ahead was an underpass, and on the right was a six-story building called the Texas School Book Depository where textbooks were stored for shipment to school districts throughout the state.

It was 12:30 P.M. when they passed the depository. Suddenly, there was a loud report, like the backfiring of an automobile exhaust.

It was a rifle shot.

Seconds later there were two more shots. A bullet had struck the President in the back. He raised his hand instinctively, then began to slump forward. Another shot caught him in the back of the head. He collapsed into Mrs. Kennedy's arms. One of the bullets

227

also hit Governor Connally below the right shoulder blade and tore through his chest.

Mrs. Kennedy was horror-stricken. Everything had happened so swiftly that she hadn't been able to utter a sound. But now she screamed in disbelief, "Oh, no! Oh, no!"

Pandemonium broke loose. Everywhere people were running and shouting. A Secret Service agent threw himself on the back of the presidential automobile to try to shield the President from further injury. The powerful Lincoln roared out of the motorcade and sped off toward Parkland Memorial Hospital, four miles away.

Mrs. Kennedy cradled the President's head in her lap. When they got to the hospital, she helped the attendants transfer him to a stretcher. She did not cry or say a word. While her husband was being wheeled to an emergency room, she held his hand. Governor Connally, too, was taken from the car and prepared for immediate surgery.

The President was placed on an operating table, and a team of physicians went to work at frantic speed. After a few minutes, they realized the hopelessness of the situation. It was too late.

John Fitzgerald Kennedy was dead at forty-six, the victim of an assassin's bullets. He had been President for two years, ten months and two days.

Two priests who had been hastily summoned to the hospital proceeded to administer the last rites. Mrs. Kennedy bent down, kissed her husband's cheek and took his hand in both of hers and pressed it against her face.

Vice-President Johnson and Mrs. Johnson had followed the presidential car to the hospital. Informed of the President's death, Mr. Johnson, though visibly shaken, immediately took charge of the situation. He instructed that an announcement on the outcome of the tragedy be made to the army of newsmen gathered outside.

An hour and a half later, Lyndon Baines Johnson was sworn in as President while standing in the cabin of "Air Force One." A casket containing John F. Kennedy's body was already aboard. Mrs. Kennedy, pale and dazed, was present during the brief ceremony. Her skirt and stockings were smeared with her fallen husband's blood. After the brief ceremony, the presidential jet took off immediately for Washington.

Meanwhile, in Dallas, police had arrested Lee Harvey Oswald, a twenty-year-old former Marine and a Marxist sympathizer, for the assassination of the President. Oswald, who had worked in the Texas School Book Depository, had been seen fleeing the scene right after the murder. A short time later, a man answering his description was stopped two miles away from the assassination scene for questioning by Dallas patrolman J. D. Tippit. The man pulled out a revolver and shot the policeman dead.

Cornered at last in a movie theatre six blocks from where the second murder had taken place, Oswald reached for a pistol concealed in his shirt, but he was subdued and captured before he could use it.

In Washington, "Air Force One" was met by Attorney-General Robert Kennedy and a small army of grief-stricken officials. The heavy bronze casket containing the late President's body was removed from the plane and taken from the airfield in a naval ambulance.

The magic of modern communications had sped the

word of the catastrophe to every corner of the world. Throughout the United States people wept openly, as if a close member of their own family had been taken from them. The radio and television networks suspended all commercial broadcasting in deference to the late President's memory.

But the expressions of sorrow were not restricted to Americans. In France, men and women cried unashamedly in the streets. A Russian woman announcer in Moscow, while narrating a television broadcast about John F. Kennedy's career, paused to choke back tears. Mrs. Khrushchev, wife of the Soviet Premier, cried. So did Italy's President. And in the Vatican, Pope Paul knelt and offered a special prayer for the soul of the assassinated President.

In churches in virtually every country of the world special memorial services were held to honor the martyred President. Because of the miracle of radio and television, it was an expression of world-wide sorrow such as had not been seen before in the whole history of mankind.

On Sunday, November 24, two days after the President's death, a shocking, almost unbelievable, sequel occurred in Texas. While being transferred from the Dallas jailhouse to the county jail, Lee Harvey Oswald was himself shot and killed by an agitated fifty-year-old night club owner, Jack Ruby, who claimed he had sought to avenge the President's death. With the murder of Oswald, it seemed that the mystery surrounding the assassination of John F. Kennedy would probably never be cleared up.

However, there was good news from Texas, too. The doctors announced that Governor John Connally would recover from his bullet wounds.

In Washington, the casket of the dead President was taken to the great rotunda of the Capitol and placed in the custody of an honor guard of servicemen. It lay on the same catafalque on which Abraham Lincoln had lain in state following his assassination a century before. During brief ceremonies, Mrs. Kennedy knelt and gently kissed the American flag that covered the casket. Caroline, also kneeling, fumbled tenderly under the flag with her hand to reach just a little bit closer to her father.

Afterward, the rotunda was opened to the general public. For the next eighteen hours, Americans of every age, race and creed wandered sorrowfully past the bier in silent tribute. Some waited as long as ten hours, and the line of mourners stretched for more than three miles. The steady shuffle of feet continued all during the day and throughout the night.

They had come from all corners of the nation to pay their final respects to their fallen President. Some had come to Washington by plane; others had arrived by train or bus or automobile. A few had even bicycled to the capital. In all, more than two hundred and fifty thousand people passed through the rotunda to mourn the husband, father and world leader who had been cut down in the prime of life—a young man who had had so much to live for.

On the morning of Monday, November 25, the President's casket was taken from the rotunda and carried down the Capitol steps by nine pallbearers representing all the services. It was placed on an artillery caisson and drawn along Pennsylvania Avenue by three pairs of matched gray horses. The route was the exact reverse of that taken by the President three years before, during his inaugural parade. Following military custom, the right row of horses was saddled but rider-less, while three members of the cavalry rode in the left row.

It was a day of dazzling brilliance. Just behind the artillery caisson an officer led a great black riderless horse, carrying empty boots reversed in the stirrups, signifying that the warrior would never again mount the steed. It was a tradition as old as Genghis Khan.

Along the sidewalks, crowds of silent, grief-stricken people gathered, many weeping, others standing silent and glum. The cadence of the march was beaten out on muffled drums to the accompaniment of sad dirges played on shrill bagpipes. In the funeral cortege were the leaders of many of the nations of the world who had flown in to pay homage to the President as he was laid to rest.

The casket was carried up the steps of St. Matthew's Cathedral, followed by Mrs. Kennedy and the other members of the Kennedy family, with the exception of Joseph P. Kennedy who was still immobilized from the stroke he had suffered two years before. The Am-bassador had been told of the tragedy and had accepted the news with quiet stoicism.

Richard Cardinal Cushing celebrated the Mass in his harsh Boston voice. He intoned, "Hail Mary, full of grace . . ." Mrs. Kennedy, with Caroline beside her, listened and began to weep softly. Afterward, the coffin was taken outside and placed on the caisson again. Three-year-old John-John saluted as he stood beside his mother. Mrs. Kennedy had regained her composure now, and was no longer crying.

The ride to Arlington National Cemetery took an hour. The sun was so bright and warm that even the cold air seemed to have softened a bit. Soon they left

Washington and the Lincoln Memorial behind and were crossing the Potomac.

Except for the sound of creaking caisson wheels and clattering hoofs, the procession entered Arlington in silence. It passed the graves of American war heroes and headed for a burial spot on a grassy hill which overlooked the tranquil Potomac.

The graveside service did not last long. Fifty jet fighters roared over the cemetery in salute. "Air Force One," the presidential plane, passed overhead, dipping its wings in farewell. There were final prayers and the sad sound of taps. A rifle volley cracked out a tribute.

Mrs. Kennedy stepped forward and lighted an eternal flame which had been set up near the grave at her request. She could not seem to get out of her mind the lines from the song her husband had loved: *"Don't let it be forgot that once there was a spot, for one brief shining moment that was known as Camelot."* Then, accompanied by Robert Kennedy, she walked slowly down the little hill, holding herself proud and erect, as she knew the President would have wanted her to.

Through his deeds and words, John F. Kennedy continues to live in the hearts of free men everywhere. His spirit—the spirit of the New Frontier—is not stilled. He is remembered by some as a young man touched with romance who released the idealistic impulses of a generation. Others honor him as the peacemaker who helped show humanity how to take a bold first step in the thousand-mile journey toward nuclear disarmament and international peace. He is remembered by still others as the young champion who fought to uphold for everyone, regardless of race or creed, the rights guaranteed to all men by a democratic society.

On Election Eve in 1960, John F. Kennedy had spoken eloquently at the Boston Garden. Pointing a finger at the audience, he declared in a sharp, clear voice, "I run for the Presidency of the United States because it is the center of action and, in a free society, the chief responsibility of the President is to set before the American people the unfinished business of our country."

The unfinished business of the country—and of the world—is the challenge John F. Kennedy placed before the people of the United States. The spirit of adventure and a determination necessary to meet that challenge comprise his legacy to the nation he loved and served.

BIBLIOGRAPHY

Burns, James MacGregor. *John Kennedy: A Political Profile*. New York: Harcourt, Brace & Company, 1959.

Carr, William H. A. *JFK: An Informal Biography*. New York: Lancer Books, Inc., 1962.

Donovan, Robert J. *PT 109: John F. Kennedy in World War II*. New York: McGraw-Hill Book Company, Inc., 1961.

Fuller, Helen. *Year of Trial: Kennedy's Crucial Decisions*. New York: Harcourt, Brace & World, Inc., 1962.

Gardner, Gerald, editor. *The Quotable Mr. Kennedy*. New York: Abelard-Schuman Limited, 1962.

Hilsman, Roger. *To Move a Nation: The Politics of Foreign Policy in the Administration of John F. Kennedy*. Garden City, N. Y.: Doubleday & Company, Inc., 1967.

Kennedy, John F. *Profiles in Courage*. New York: Harper & Brothers, 1956.

———. *The Strategy of Peace*. Edited by Allan Nevins. New York: Harper & Brothers, 1960.

———. *To Turn the Tide*. Edited by John W. Gardner. New York: Harper & Brothers, 1962.

———. *Why England Slept*. New York: Wilfred Funk, Inc., 1940.

Let Us Begin: The First 100 Days of the Kennedy Administration. New York: Simon and Schuster, 1961.

Lowe, Jacques. *Portrait: The Emergence of John F. Ken-

nedy. New York: McGraw-Hill Book Company, Inc., 1961.

McCarthy, Joe. *The Remarkable Kennedys*. New York: The Dial Press, 1960.

Manchester, William. *Portrait of a President*. Boston: Little, Brown and Company, 1962.

Manshester, William Raymond. *The Death of a President*. New York: Harper & Row, Publishers, 1967.

Markmann, Charles Lam and Mark Sherwin. *John F. Kennedy: A Sense of Purpose*. New York: St. Martin's Press, 1961.

Michener, James A. *Report of the County Chairman*. New York: Random House, 1961.

Opotowsky, Stan. *The Kennedy Government*. New York: E. P. Dutton Co., Inc., 1961.

Schlesinger, Arthur M., Jr. *A Thousand Days: John F. Kennedy in the White House*. Boston: Houghton Mifflin Company, 1965.

Shannon, William Vincent. *The Heir Apparent: Robert Kennedy and the Struggle for Power*. New York: The Macmillan Company, 1967.

Sidey, Hugh. *John F. Kennedy, President*. New York: Atheneum, 1964.

Sorensen, Theodore. *Kennedy*. New York: Harper & Row, Publishers, 1965.

Tregaskis, Richard. *John F. Kennedy: War Hero*. New York: Random House, 1962.

Whalen, Richard J. *The Founding Father: The Story of Joseph P. Kennedy*. New York: The New American Library, Inc., 1964.

Whipple, Chandler. *Lt. John F. Kennedy—Expendable*. New York: Universal Publishing and Distributing Corporation, 1962.

White, Theodore H. *The Making of the President 1960*. New York: Atheneum, 1961.

INDEX

ARCHWAY
PAPERBACKS

Other titles you will enjoy

29054 WHITE WATER, STILL WATER, by J. Allan Bosworth. Illustrated by Charles W. Walker. Swept down river on a raft, Chris faces a hazardous journey home through the wilderness —barefoot and equipped with nothing but a broken-bladed pocketknife. (50¢)

29047 HAUNTED SUMMER, by Hope Dahle Jordan. When the newspaper headlines screamed *Hit and Run Driver,* Rilla became a hunted and haunted person as she desperately tried to hide the secret of her involvement in the accident. (50¢)

29056 THE STORY OF PHILLIS WHEATLEY: *Poetess of the American Revolution,* by Shirley Graham. The moving story of the brilliant, young Afro-American whose poetry won her recognition in America and England and praise from Tom Paine and General George Washington. (50¢)

29013 THE DEVIL AND DANIEL WEBSTER *and Other Stories,* by Stephen Vincent Benét. Illustrated by Harold Denison and Charles Child. Three short stories by the American master of fantasy, folk humor, and irresistible tall tales. (50¢)

29048 JUNIOR MISS, by Sally Benson. The heart-warming and hilarious adventures of the one and only Judy Graves as she tackles the joys and heartaches of growing up. (50¢)

29035 THE SILENT STORM, by Marion Marsh Brown and Ruth Crone. Illustrated by Fritz Kredel. The moving story of Annie Sullivan, the courageous teacher of Helen Keller, and how she emerged from her own childhood of despair and poverty to become the kind of woman who stood up to life and refused to let it defeat her. (50¢)

29036 KEEPER OF THE WILD BULLS, by Heinz Sponsel. Translated by Hertha Pauli. Illustrated by Helmar Becker-Berke. Pierre wins a glorious year of freedom herding the fierce, fighting bulls on the vast plains of southern France. (50¢)

29015 THE JIM THORPE STORY: *America's Greatest Athlete,* by Gene Schoor. Illustrated with photographs. The greatest all-around athlete of this century and his spectacular record in football, baseball, field and track. (50¢)

29043 CAPTAIN OF THE PLANTER: *The Story of Robert Smalls,* by Dorothy Sterling. Illustrated by Ernest Crichlow. A stirring biography of the Negro Civil War hero who became a congressman during Reconstruction and fought courageously for civil rights. (50¢)

(If your bookseller does not have the titles you want, you may order them by sending the retail price, plus 15¢ per book for postage and handling to: Mail Service Department, Washington Square Press, a division of Simon & Schuster, Inc., 1 West 39th Street, New York, N. Y. 10018. Please enclose check or money order—do not send cash.)

Seventeenth Summer

by MAUREEN DALY

"...an enchanting book—one which rings true and sweet and fresh and sound...."

Angie Morrow and Jack Duluth went out together for the first time in June. Most of their dates that summer of Angie's seventeenth year followed a familiar pattern—Cokes at the drugstore with the crowd, rides in Jack's jalopy, movies. But, as the weeks slipped by and their love grew, the drowsy golden summer became more and more enchanted....

"...Simply, eloquently, Maureen Daly tells one how youth in love really feels—how it felt yesterday and how it feels today."

—THE NEW YORK TIMES

There is a magic and wonder in first love that can never be felt a second time. Maureen Daly, who was barely past seventeen when she wrote her best-selling, prize-winning novel, was able to capture its ecstatic freshness with an extraordinary sensitivity no older author could touch.

#29044 ARCHWAY PAPERBACKS 50¢

WASHINGTON SQUARE PRESS

If your bookseller does not have the titles you want, you may order them by sending the retail price, plus 15¢ per book for postage and handling to: Mail Service Department, Washington Square Press, a division of Simon & Schuster, Inc., 1 West 39th Street, New York, N. Y. 10018. Please enclose check or money order—do not send cash.